T0328566

Cambridge Elements ≡

Elements in Campaigns and Elections
edited by
R. Michael Alvarez
California Institute of Technology
Emily Beaulieu Bacchus
University of Kentucky
Charles Stewart III
Massachusetts Institute of Technology

CITIZENS UNDER COMPULSORY VOTING: A THREE-COUNTRY STUDY

Ruth Dassonneville
University of Montreal

Thiago Barbosa
Brazilian Federal Senate

André Blais
University of Montreal

Ian McAllister
Australian National University

Mathieu Turgeon
Western University

CAMBRIDGE
UNIVERSITY PRESS

CAMBRIDGE
UNIVERSITY PRESS

Shaftesbury Road, Cambridge CB2 8EA, United Kingdom

One Liberty Plaza, 20th Floor, New York, NY 10006, USA

477 Williamstown Road, Port Melbourne, VIC 3207, Australia

314–321, 3rd Floor, Plot 3, Splendor Forum, Jasola District Centre, New Delhi – 110025, India

103 Penang Road, #05–06/07, Visioncrest Commercial, Singapore 238467

Cambridge University Press is part of Cambridge University Press & Assessment, a department of the University of Cambridge.

We share the University's mission to contribute to society through the pursuit of education, learning and research at the highest international levels of excellence.

www.cambridge.org
Information on this title: www.cambridge.org/9781009069120

DOI: 10.1017/9781009071116

First published 2023

A catalogue record for this publication is available from the British Library

ISBN 978-1-009-06912-0 Paperback
ISSN 2633-0970 (online)
ISSN 2633-0962 (print)

Citizens Under Compulsory Voting:
A Three-Country Study

Elements in Campaigns and Elections

DOI: 10.1017/9781009071116
First published online: August 2023

Ruth Dassonneville
University of Montreal

Thiago Barbosa
Brazilian Federal Senate

André Blais
University of Montreal

Ian McAllister
Australian National University

Mathieu Turgeon
Western University

Author for correspondence: Ruth Dassonneville, ruth.dassonneville@umontreal.ca

Abstract: A burgeoning literature studies compulsory voting and its effects on turnout, but the scholarly literature provides very few insights about how compulsory voting works in practice. In this Element, the authors fill this gap by providing an in-depth discussion of compulsory voting rules and their enforcement in Australia, Belgium, and Brazil. By analysing comparable public opinion data from these three countries, they shed light on citizens' attitudes towards compulsory voting. The Element examines citizens' perceptions, their knowledge of the system, and whether they support it. The authors connect this with information on citizens' reported turnout and vote choice to assess who is affected by mandatory voting and why. The work clarifies that there is no single system of compulsory voting. Each country has its own set of rules, and most voters are unaware of how they are enforced.

Keywords: compulsory voting, sanctions, voter turnout, political knowledge, public opinion

ISBNs: 9781009069120 (PB), 9781009071116 (OC)
ISSNs: 2633-0970 (online), 2633-0962 (print)

Contents

An Online Appendix is available at
Cambridge.org/Dassonneville

1 Introduction

In 2021, twenty-seven countries or regions had some form of compulsory voting and mandated voters to participate in elections. The list includes small countries like Liechtenstein, Luxembourg, or Nauru, but also countries with large populations like Australia, Brazil, and Mexico. Compulsory voting is found across the world, including in Africa, Asia, Europe, Latin America, and Oceania (for a list of countries, see Table 1.1 in Singh 2021). Turnout is generally high in these countries. This is a logical consequence of the fact that mandating citizens to turn out to vote is one of the most effective ways to guarantee high levels of electoral participation (Franklin 1999). While several institutional features correlate with turnout, according to Lijphart (1997: 10), '[c]ompulsory voting is the only institutional mechanism ... that can assure high turnout virtually by itself'.

Most of what we know about compulsory voting and its effects on citizens' electoral behaviour comes from large comparative analyses. Such work suffers from two important limitations. First, comparative analyses of correlates of compulsory voting, at the individual or the aggregate level, tend to rely on broad categorizations of compulsory and voluntary voting countries. At most, this work distinguishes between weak and strongly enforced compulsory voting (Panagopoulos 2008; Singh 2015). This implies an enormous loss of information, overlooking variation in the ways in which countries compel citizens to vote, what the sanctions for non-voting are, and how those are put in practice and perceived by citizens.

A second limitation of work that has taken a broad comparative perspective is its focus on gathering information about a limited number of variables across a wide range of countries. Doing so allows for studying general patterns and ascertaining differences between compulsory and voluntary voting countries. But by taking such a broad perspective previous work has neglected the dynamics of compulsory voting rules *within* countries that compel citizens to vote. This implies that we lack information on simple but key questions like: What do citizens think are the consequences of abstaining in these countries? Do citizens in these countries favour compulsory over voluntary voting? Who supports compulsory voting? Who is most affected by compulsory voting? Which voters in these countries would still vote if voting was voluntary? And what are the consequences for the political system of near-universal turnout?

This Element fills these gaps in the literature by means of an in-depth comparative analysis of citizens' perceptions of compulsory voting rules and their behaviour in three prominent compulsory voting countries: Australia, Belgium, and Brazil. We use original, representative election survey data from these three countries, in which we integrated identical questions to study comparatively citizens' perceptions of the sanctions associated with compulsory voting, their support for compulsory voting, and their electoral behaviour.

The surveys were fielded following the 2019 Australian federal election, the 2019 Belgian regional and federal elections, and between the first and second rounds of the 2018 presidential elections in Brazil. In Australia, the questions were fielded as part of the post-election study that incorporated the questions from the fifth module of the Comparative Study of Electoral Systems project (CSES). The survey was a probabilistic online survey, and it achieved a high response rate (77 per cent). In total, 2,000 respondents completed the survey. In Belgium, the questions were integrated into a probabilistic post-electoral survey organized by the Centre for Citizenship and Democracy at KU Leuven. Respondents in the two main regions of Belgium (Flanders and Wallonia) were sampled from the National Register and were sent a paper survey by regular mail. This procedure resulted in a total of 1,820 completed surveys and a response rate of 23 per cent. Finally, in Brazil, the questions were included in a non-probabilistic online survey of 5,078 respondents aged between eighteen and sixty-nine, the age group for which compulsory voting applies. The sample used quotas to match the population's sex, age, social class, and region of residence. We rely on these data for most of the analyses presented in this manuscript. For the two probability surveys – Australia and Belgium – we consistently weigh the data to account for the under- or overrepresentation of specific socio-demographic groups.

These survey data allow for a close look at how citizens in compulsory voting countries perceive and experience this system, and how it affects their electoral behaviour. We included measures to capture citizens' support for compulsory voting, their perceptions of the consequences of abstention, and whether they would turn out under voluntary voting. We present the exact survey items and their question wording in the relevant sections.

The plan for the book is as follows. In Section 2 we present our three cases, providing historical background on the introduction of compulsory voting in Australia, Belgium, and Brazil, as well as detailed information on the law and its enforcement. We then turn to an analysis of citizens' perceptions of compulsory voting, with Section 3 providing insights about citizens' perceptions of enforcement as well as to whom compulsory voting applies. In Section 4 we assess support for the institution of compulsory voting and examine the correlates of support. Section 5 zooms in on the effects of compulsory voting on turnout – with specific attention given to the role of perceptions of sanctions in mobilizing voters. We continue our assessment of the consequences of compulsory voting with a focus on its secondary effects in Section 6. In this section, we give particular attention to the role of compulsory voting in making politics and representation more equal. We end with a brief concluding section in which we summarize our main findings and expand on their implications.

2 Three Cases: Australia, Belgium, and Brazil

While all twenty-seven countries or regions worldwide that currently use some form of compulsory voting share the same goal of compelling citizens to turn out to vote in elections, there are substantial variations in implementation and enforcement. In this section, we address the specificities and historical backgrounds that led the three countries we study to adopt compulsory voting: Australia, widely regarded as a case of success; Belgium, one of the first countries to adopt compulsory voting; and Brazil, the largest democracy in the world with compulsory voting.

Australia, Belgium, and Brazil feature prominently in previous work on the effects of mandatory voting on turnout. That work has drawn attention to the fact that enforcement and the sanctions for non-voting vary substantially between these countries. Panagopoulous (2008) codes sanctions for non-voting as 'moderate' in Australia and Brazil and 'high' in Belgium. In terms of enforcement, he codes Brazil as a case of 'weak' enforcement and Australia and Belgium as settings where enforcement is 'strict'. In line with this coding, Singh (2011) uses a 4-point scale to capture the severity of compulsory voting (from 0 for voluntary systems to a maximum of 4) and gives Brazil a score of 2, Australia 3, and Belgium 4. In more recent work, Singh (2021) classifies the severity of penalties and enforcement in compulsory voting in Australia, Belgium, and Brazil as 'medium'.

It is worth mentioning that the variation in measurement observed in previous work may reflect not only variation and changes in rules and enforcement over time in the three countries but also encompass methodological differences. While Panagopoulos (2008) measures sanctions and enforcement separately, Singh (2010, 2021) combines both dimensions in a single classification. More importantly, the authors rely on different data sources; Panagopoulos sources information from the International Institute for Democracy and Electoral Assistance (IDEA) and Singh (2021) relies on information from the Varieties of Democracy (V-Dem) project.

Next, we offer more details about the history of mandatory voting in Australia, Belgium, and Brazil. We indicate when compulsory voting was adopted, the main justifications for its implementation, and how the public and the political elites received it. We then discuss the effects of compulsory voting on turnout and its support in each society. Finally, we address the enrolment and enforcement rules, emphasizing who is obliged to vote and the penalties for those citizens who fail to comply. As we will see, enforcement is generally less strict in practice than prescribed by the law, and voters are often unaware of this disjunction.

2.1 Australia

Compulsory voting was introduced for Commonwealth (federal) elections in 1924, but its origins can be traced back to the system of compulsory enrolment, which was implemented for Commonwealth elections in 1911. Making enrolment compulsory was intended to rationalize the electoral roll and reduce the administrative costs of ensuring that it remains up to date (Bennett 2005; Mackerras and McAllister 1999). Once compulsory enrolment was introduced, implementing compulsory voting was regarded as a natural next step (Hirst 2002: 114).

In 1915, compulsory voting was considered for a proposed referendum (Evans 2006). The referendum never took place, but the debate that it generated set compulsory voting in motion (Fowler 2013: 163). Queensland was the first jurisdiction to introduce compulsory voting, also in 1915. The policy was implemented by the Liberal government of Digby Denhan on the premise that it would create a level playing field, as the opposing Labor Party was deemed more efficient in 'getting out the vote' (Evans 2006). Ironically, Denham lost the 1915 election to the Labor Party – which objected to the policy at first. That was the only time compulsory voting in Australia faced any party opposition (Fowler 2013: 162).

The decline in turnout observed in the 1922 election, when less than 60 per cent of registered voters turned out to vote – compared to more than 71 per cent at the 1919 election – may have been the catalyst for the adoption of compulsory voting at the federal level (Evans 2006). This decline concerned both parties and their members believed that they would personally benefit from compulsory voting (Gow 1971: 209). As a result, the Commonwealth followed Queensland in 1924. The remaining states would eventually adhere to compulsory voting. Victoria adopted it in 1926. Next came Tasmania and New South Wales in 1928 and Western Australia in 1936. The last state to adopt it was South Australia in 1941.

In every jurisdiction, the move to introduce compulsory voting attracted unanimous support from all parties. This massive support likely stemmed from practical reasons (Fowler 2013: 163–4), as the new system suited the political parties. Compulsory voting would reduce the time and effort needed to mobilize the vote and lower campaign expenditures (Gow 1971; McAllister 1986), and the fines collected could also alleviate the administrative costs associated with organizing elections in a large country (Mackerras and McAllister 1999: 220). Moreover, both the Labor Party and the two Coalition parties aimed to offset what they perceived as an advantage enjoyed by their rival (Mackerras and McAllister 1999). The Labor Party could rely on a substantial number of voluntary campaign workers who would bring Labor voters to the polls. On the other hand, right-wing Coalition voters were more likely to own cars, making it easier for them and their partisans to access the polls (Fowler 2013; Hirst 2002). Both sides therefore preferred to concentrate resources on voter conversion.

The effect on turnout was impressive and instantaneous, as will be detailed in Section 5. In the six states and the Commonwealth, an average 23 percentage points increase in turnout was observed. The most modest growth, of 13 percentage points, was registered in Queensland. In contrast, in South Australia, turnout went from 51 per cent to 89 per cent, an increase of 38 percentage points (Mackerras and McAllister 1999). As illustrated in Figure 1, in the first Commonwealth election after the adoption of compulsion, in 1925, turnout

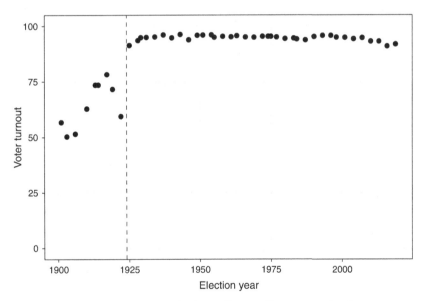

Figure 1 Voter turnout in Australian parliamentary elections
from 1945 to 2019

Note: The scatter points indicate voter turnout (as a per cent of registered voters) in federal elections. Data between 1901 and 2016 come from Barber (2016). Data for 2019 are from the International Institute for Democracy and Electoral Assistance – IDEA (www.idea.int/data-tools/country-view/68/40). The dashed vertical line indicates when compulsory voting was adopted. Detailed turnout rates are shown in online Appendix A.

was 91 per cent, an increase of 32 percentage points over the previous election (Barber 2016: 7). Since 1924, turnout in the House of Representatives has consistently remained above 90 per cent and has usually been higher. In the 2019 election, it was 92 per cent.

Compulsory voting in Australia works as follows: all citizens aged eighteen years and over who are on the electoral roll are required to attend the poll on election day or to cast their vote under one of the many available options, including postal voting, absent voting, or voting at mobile polling facilities set up by the Australian Electoral Commission (AEC) in prisons, remote areas, hospitals, and nursing homes (Evans 2006). Within three months of polling day, the returning officer in each electorate (constituency) is required to send a penalty notice to each voter who did not have their name noted on the register. The voter has the option of providing a valid reason under the legislation for not voting. Although there is no fixed, comprehensive list of these reasons, they typically include, among other things, religion, travel, or illness. If a valid reason is not provided, the voter may either pay an administrative penalty (currently A$20, though it is higher for some state elections) or have the matter dealt with in court.

In practice, the AEC accepts any reasonable explanation for not voting. In the 2004 election, for instance, the AEC issued 458,952 non-voter notices and received almost 300,000 replies from 'apparent non-voters'. The AEC considered only about 3 per cent of these replies as not valid. Only a fraction of the invalid replies (1,092) received a penalty notice, while most (8,326) were just issued a warning (Bennett 2005: 27). The number of citizens who choose to take the matter to court is even smaller – Bennett (2005) reports there were only 7 in 2004. Many voters (more than 50,000 in 2004, about 11 per cent of the notices issued) opt to pay the fine right away instead of presenting reasons for not voting. Finally, because states' electoral commissions are independent agencies, their criteria for accepting the reasons provided by non-voters may vary. The proportion of non-voters who are fined therefore varies for state elections. The Victorian Electoral Commission, for instance, sanctioned more than half of the voters who were issued a notice after the 2014 state election (Victorian Electoral Commission 2015).

2.2 Belgium

Belgium was one of the first countries to introduce compulsory voting and the first one where the obligation to vote was extended nationally. It did so in 1893 when universal suffrage was granted (to men).[1] Ever since, the Belgian constitution stipulates that voting is compulsory. At the time, there were three main

---

[1] Female suffrage was granted in 1948, at which point voting became compulsory for women as well (Meier 2012).

justifications for the adoption of compulsory voting. First, the self-evident desire to improve election turnout (Kuzelewska 2016). Reuchamps et al. (2018) indicate that before the introduction of compulsory voting, turnout in legislative elections varied substantially, regularly dropping below 70 per cent and with an absolute low of 62 per cent in 1868. Turnout was even lower in provincial and local elections. By making voting mandatory, workers' movements – including the new Socialist Workers Party – wanted to 'prevent employers from denying the workers the right to vote by detaining them at work' (Kuzelewska 2016: 40). The Liberal Party, in contrast, opposed compulsory voting based on the argument that abstainers lacked genuine interest and were incapable of casting an informed vote (Malkopolou 2014: 1).

A second reason for introducing compulsory voting was to limit the electoral impact of radical parties. The mainstream Catholic party hoped that compulsory voting would increase its vote in rural areas – countering the rise of new 'radical' parties in the urban centres (Kuzelewska 2016). It was generally assumed that voters who held extreme ideological positions were more inclined to vote. By mandating moderates to turn out, the influence of more extreme voters would be attenuated (Reuchamps et al. 2018).

Third, political elites favoured compulsory voting to diminish the efforts and expenditures related to the mobilization of voters. Stengers (1990) mentions that candidates motivated voters to come to the polls by reimbursing their travel expenses or compensating them with food. To avoid mobilization costs following the introduction of universal suffrage, political elites sought to limit their expenses by mandating voting instead of mobilizing them (Kuzelewska 2016; Reuchamps et al. 2018). The introduction of compulsory voting in Belgium accomplished its primary aim, as levels of abstention dropped considerably. This is shown in Figure 2, which plots voter turnout rates for Belgian parliamentary elections as reported by Bouhon and Reuchamps (2018). Only 7 per cent of eligible voters abstained in the 1894 election after the passage of compulsory voting, as compared to 27 per cent and 16 per cent in the two preceding elections, respectively.

The rule, which can best be described as an obligation to go to the polls on election day – and thus as compulsory participation rather than compulsory voting (Deschouwer 2012) – applies to all citizens registered at an address in Belgium. These citizens are automatically registered as voters when they reach the voting age of eighteen years.[2] For Belgians living abroad, registration is

---

[2] From 2024 onwards, the voting age for European Parliament elections will be lowered to sixteen in Belgium. In contrast to those who are older than eighteen-, sixteen- and seventeen-year-olds will not be automatically included on the voting rolls. Voluntary registration implies that voting will remain voluntary for those who are under eighteen (De Kamer 2021).

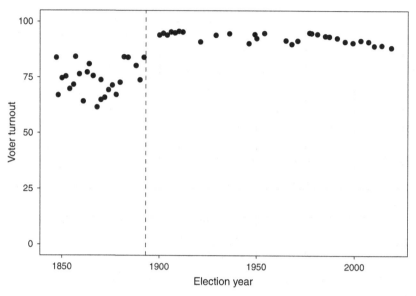

Figure 2 Voter turnout in Belgian parliamentary elections
from 1847 to 2019

Note: The scatter points indicate voter turnout (as a per cent of registered voters) in federal elections. The dashed vertical line indicates when compulsory voting was adopted. Source: Bouhon and Reuchamps (2018), Annexe 2. Data for 2019 come from IDEA (www.idea.int/data-tools/country-view/60/40). Detailed estimates are shown in online Appendix A.

optional, but once registered they are obliged to vote as well. Similar rules apply to non-Belgians living in Belgium for a minimum of five years, who are eligible to vote in municipal elections (Pilet 2007). All elections held since 1893, at different levels of government, have been held under compulsory voting rules. This will change in 2024, when municipal and provincial elections in the Flemish region will be held under voluntary voting rules for the first time since the late nineteenth century. This change followed a majority vote[3] in the Flemish parliament in July 2021 to abolish compulsory voting in provincial and municipal elections in Flanders. In other regions, as well as in elections for regional, federal, and European elections (which are all organized by the federal administration), voting remains compulsory.

According to the federal compulsory voting law, citizens who abstain from voting without a valid excuse risk are reprimanded or face a monetary fine

---

[3] The centre-right government that supported the decree is comprised by N-VA (New Flemish Alliance), CD&V (Christian Democratic and Flemish) and Open Vld (Open Flemish Liberals and Democrats). The opposition is formed by Vlaams Belang, Groen, Vooruit (Forward, formerly named SP.a) and PVDA (Workers' Party of Belgium).

between 40 and 80 euros, depending on the circumstances. For those who repeatedly abstain, the fine increases in value somewhere between 80 and 200 euros. Finally, those abstaining four times without a valid excuse in a fifteen-year time window risk being removed from the electoral rolls for a period of ten years. Removal from the electoral rolls excludes citizens from being appointed to or promoted by a public authority (VRT Nieuws 2018).

Although the law stipulates sanctions for non-voting, in recent years compulsory voting in Belgium has not been enforced. In practice, the responsible judge in a Judicial District receives the names of citizens within their jurisdiction who abstained from voting without a valid excuse.[4] Valid reasons for not voting include illness, being abroad on election day, and fundamental objections (Engelen 2005). Then, the judge decides whether to follow up on these voting law violations. Engelen (2005) mentions that following the 1999 elections, 332 out of 692,670 non-voters (i.e., less than 0.5 per cent) were prosecuted. Prosecutions were often not universally carried out, but rather the initiative of a single judge, as in the judicial District of Mechelen, where about 1,000 voters were reprimanded for abstaining in the 2000 local elections (De Standaard 2001).

While judges would occasionally reprimand abstainers in some judicial districts, prosecuting non-voters is not a priority for the courts, and no fines have been issued to non-voters in recent years.[5] In 2003, the Minister of Justice asked the judiciary not to prioritize the reprimanding of abstainers (Vlaamse Overheid 2021). In 2012, Annemie Turtelboom – in her capacity as the federal Minister of Justice – went further by explicitly asking public prosecutors *not* to reprimand abstainers. It was also communicated publicly that abstainers would not receive a fine. She did, however, ask to prosecute citizens who were designated as chairs or assessors at the polling station but did not show up (Senate 2012).

The lack of enforcement of the law is one of the main arguments used by those opposing compulsory voting (Vlaamse Overheid 2021). Without enforcement, why keep the law at all? An additional argument – which liberal parties tend to use – is that mandating voting is not a good instrument to strengthen democracy because it relies on the mobilization of citizens who lack any interest in politics. Liberal members of Parliament, at different levels of government,

---

[4] Citizens who anticipate that they will not be able to turn out to vote have the option to send their motivation to the judiciary before election day. They can also opt to vote by proxy.

[5] The last election for which sources indicate some voters have been fined is 2007. About 12 out of approximately 690,000 abstainers have been asked to pay a fine (Sudinfo 2014). These are estimates, based on research in the context of the 2007 election. Unfortunately, statistics are not centrally collected or maintained over time (personal communication with the Belgian Criminal Policy Department).

have on several occasions submitted bills to abolish compulsory voting. Apart from the recently voted law to shift to voluntary voting for local elections in the Flemish region, such efforts have never found majority support. At the federal level, the Francophone Socialist Party (PS) has been the main veto-player preventing further reform (Hooghe and Deschouwer 2011).

2.3 Brazil

Compulsory voting was first introduced in Brazil by the 1932 Electoral Code, amidst a period of significant institutional changes. The code was one of the earliest acts of the provisional government headed by Getúlio Vargas, who led the 1930 *coup d'état* that brought down the First Republic (Ricci and Zulini 2017).

The First Republic, also known as the Old Republic, lasted from 1889 to 1930. It was characterized by high levels of political and electoral decentralization. Fraud, manipulation, and even violence were standard features, particularly in rural areas (Love 1970), and elections were often just a *facade* to confirm previous intra-elite agreements (Ricci and Zulini 2017: 58). Moreover, due to several legal restrictions (mainly the exclusion of women and illiterates), less than 10 per cent of the adult population was eligible to vote (Oliveira 1999:144), and about half of them effectively turned out to vote.

The revolution of 1930 sought to redress the electoral process, among other things. The electoral code of 1932 adopted compulsory voting to increase turnout (Zulini and Ricci 2020: 604) and raise the legitimacy of the electoral process (Oliveira 1999: 144). This legislation also brought other measures to expand participation and reduce electoral fraud, including secret voting, women's suffrage, proportional representation, and the creation of an electoral court of national jurisdiction. Voting was made compulsory for citizens twenty-one and older. Even though women were allowed to vote, it was only mandatory for those who worked as public servants. Married women needed formal consent from their husbands, whereas single women and widows had to provide proof of income. The military and the illiterates were not allowed to vote. The 1932 electoral code marked an essential step toward consolidating Brazilian democracy, but this path would prove far from linear. During the following decades, Brazil experienced cycles of authoritarianism, democratization, and (re)democratization (Rios 2020).

Compulsory voting was generally well-received by the public and political elites. Its immediate effects on turnout, however, were not easy to grasp for two reasons. First, the newly created electoral court faced operational difficulties in re-enrolling citizens and issuing new voter registration cards after revoking previous electoral registers. This administrative difficulty helps to explain the *decrease* in turnout observed in the 1933 election, the first to be held under the new electoral code. Second and most importantly, in a self-coup in 1937, Vargas proclaimed the 'New State' (*Estado Novo*), an authoritarian regime that dissolved the electoral court, shut down Congress, and suppressed political parties and elections. Brazilians would only be able to vote again after the overthrow of Vargas' regime in 1945.

The 1945 presidential elections are often regarded as the first actual competitive, democratic elections held in Brazil (Bethell 2000: 8). Voting remained compulsory, and the voting age was lowered to 18. Voter turnout was high, at 83 per cent, but registered voters accounted for less than a quarter of the voting-age population.

In 1964, Brazilian democracy was once again interrupted by a military coup. Even during the military dictatorship (1964–85), elections were regularly held. The president, state governors, and mayors of state capitals were chosen indirectly by the military regime, but citizens retained the right to vote in most mayoral elections (for both mayors and city council members) and for members of Congress. Even so, the regime would resort to 'political engineering' (Power and Roberts 1995: 802) whenever the popular vote threatened its interests, in a peculiar system of elections without democracy (Bethell 2000).

Currently, Brazil is the fourth largest democracy globally and the largest one to use a system of compulsory voting (Katz and Levin 2018). Voting is mandatory for all literate citizens between eighteen and sixty-nine years of age and for all electoral races. Citizens aged sixteen, seventeen, or older than sixty-nine, those who are illiterate or Indigenous have the right to vote, although they are not compelled by law to do so. Voters must vote in person in the district of their residence on election day. Voting by proxy or by mail is not allowed. Brazilians living abroad are also required to vote but only in presidential elections and can do so at a Brazilian consulate or embassy.

Citizens who fail to vote must pay a small fine (currently less than US$1) or justify their abstention before an electoral judge. In the 2020 municipal elections, citizens were allowed to justify their abstention through a mobile application due to the Covid-19 pandemic. Note, however, that abstainers in Brazil do not receive an official notification from the electoral commission after the election, like in Australia. Regardless, all sanctions are active and operational. Citizens who abstained from voting are only reminded of their pending business with the electoral justice when they need a state service – like renewing a document.

Voters who do not justify their abstention are subject to several penalties like not being able to apply for public sector jobs, receive payments from a public entity, obtain or renew a passport or identity card, enrol in a public education institution, obtain a loan from a public bank, and other restrictions. A voter with three consecutive unexcused abstentions or failures to pay the fines loses their voting rights until the situation is remedied. For elections with two rounds, each round counts as an election.

Despite this array of penalties, it is relatively simple for abstainers to remedy the situation. First, the electoral court accepts most justifications. In local and federal elections held from 2014 to 2020, almost 99 per cent of the justifications were accepted (Superior Electoral Court 2023). Moreover, even if the justification gets rejected, only a small fine has to be paid.

From the implementation of compulsory voting in 1932 to today, Brazil has experienced significant political and institutional transformations. Its electorate has changed drastically due to rapid population growth, intense urbanization, and more comprehensive enrolment rules (Bethell 2000: 8–9). From 1945 to 2018, the number of registered voters rose from 7 to 147 million, and voting-age turnout grew threefold, from 23 per cent to 76 per cent (see online Appendix A for details). Since 1989, turnout is always close to 80 per cent (Figure 3).

Even though most Brazilians do not currently support compulsory voting, as will be detailed in Section 4, there is little party support for voluntary voting. In 2015, however, when a proposition to amend the Constitution was submitted, one of the right-wing parties (DEM – Democrats) proposed to abolish compulsory

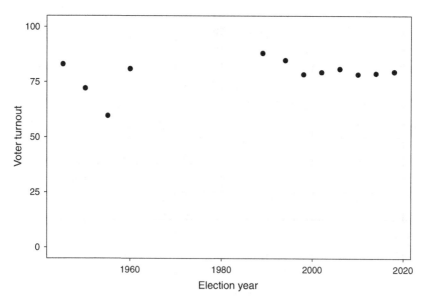

Figure 3 Voter turnout in Brazilian presidential elections from 1945 to 2018

Note: Data come from the IDEA (www.idea.int/data-tools/country-view/68/40). Detailed estimates are shown in online Appendix A.

voting. The proposal was rejected by the plenary of the Chamber of Deputies by 311 votes to 134 (Agência Câmara 2015).[6]

2.4 Summary and Implications

In this section, we explored the historical circumstances that led Australia, Belgium, and Brazil to adopt and maintain mandatory voting. We briefly presented the particularities in implementation, sanctions, enforcement, and support of compulsory voting in each country. These distinctions, which will be discussed in the following sections, are summarized in Table 1.

The context and motivations for introducing compulsory voting differ markedly in the three countries. In Australia, compulsory voting was adopted with little discussion and was regarded as a logical extension to the system of compulsory enrolment that would benefit the major political parties. In Belgium too different parties thought the introduction of compulsory voting would benefit them and would reduce the costs of election campaigns. Another common theme was the incentive among the major political parties to stem support for radical parties and groups who were attracting significant electoral support. Still, there was more debate among the political parties in Belgium than in Australia. In Brazil, the introduction of compulsory voting was complicated by interruptions to democracy; when democracy was restored, it appeared logical to implement the system that had existed before the breakdown. As a result, compulsory voting is weakly institutionalized in that country and there has not been much debate about its merits.

Although the link between compulsory voting and turnout is well established in the literature, the particularities of implementation and enforcement in each country should not be neglected. Each of the three countries has, in theory, a system of strict enforcement, but in Belgium penalties for not voting in recent elections have not been enforced. In Australia there is a consistent and strict enforcement of compulsory voting, even though the electoral commission accepts most excuses for abstaining. The Brazilian approach is fundamentally different from the Australian one. Instead of receiving a letter after the election and facing a sanction, the Brazilian abstainer is not notified by the authorities. In what could be described as passive enforcement, all sanctions are fully implemented and operational, but abstainers may only realize this when they need some state service, for example, when they want to renew a passport. This nuanced analysis of the contextual differences in compulsory voting will inform

---

[6] Other propositions to abolish compulsory voting were submitted recently, but they were filed before even reaching the voting stage (Agência Senado 2017).

Table 1 Summary of compulsory voting rules and enforcement in Australia, Belgium, and Brazil

Country	Year of introduction	Sanctions	Who must vote	Enforcement	Turnout in last election
Australia	1924	Fine (A$20).	All citizens aged eighteen years and over who are on the electoral roll.	Non-voters receive a penalty note within 3 months after the election.	91.9%
Belgium	1893	Fine (€40 to €80). Removal from the Electoral Roll.	All citizens registered at an address in Belgium are automatically registered as voters when they reach eighteen years. Belgians abroad and non-Belgians are not automatically registered but are obliged to vote when they are registered.	No enforcement since the mid-2000s.	88.4%
Brazil	1932	Fine (R$3.51, less than US$1). Inability to apply for public sector jobs, receive payments from a public entity or remuneration as a public servant, obtain or renew a passport or identity card, enrol in a public education institution, obtain a loan from a public bank, among others.	Literate citizens between eighteen and sixty-nine years. Citizens aged sixteen, seventeen, older than seventy, illiterate or Indigenous have the right, but not the obligation to vote.	There is no notification, but all sanctions are operational until the situation is remedied.	79.7%

Note: Authors' own summary based on the description presented in Section 2.

our subsequent analyses of citizens' perceptions of compulsory voting and its effect on turnout and election outcomes.

3 Citizens' Perceptions and Knowledge

The previous section has shown that there is much variation in the sanctions for abstention between Australia, Belgium, and Brazil. In each case, however, the cost for non-voting is, in practice, small or even nil. In Australia, most reasonable excuses for non-voting are accepted. In Belgium, there has not been an enforcement of the sanctions for abstainers in recent elections. And in Brazil, while enforcement is relatively strict, the financial penalties for not voting are minimal (and can be paid online).

Citizens, however, are known to be poorly informed and even misinformed about politics (Delli Carpini and Keeter 1996; Kuklinski et al. 2001), including about compulsory voting laws. Turgeon and Blais (2021), for example, show that most Brazilians know that voting is compulsory for voters aged eighteen to – seventy but that many are unsure about how the age criterion applies exactly in practice. This lack of knowledge carries important implications, as many voters cast a ballot on election day believing that they are required to vote by law although they are not legally required to do so.

In this section, we examine citizens' perceptions of the consequences of non-voting and compare them with what the law and practice tell us in Australia, Belgium, and Brazil. We also explore whether political interest meaningfully affects these perceptions. We then evaluate knowledge about compulsory voting in Brazil, with a focus on who is required to vote by law.

3.1 Citizens' Perceptions about the Consequences of Abstaining

We integrated a series of questions about the perceptions of the consequences of non-voting in each of the three election surveys, as discussed in Section 1. We designed these questions so that they could be applied uniformly in Australia, Belgium, and Brazil. Specifically, we asked respondents who indicated that they had voted in the last election:

To the best of your knowledge, if you had not voted in the election, would you have to ... ?
1. Fill in a form
2. Go to court
3. Pay a fine

For each item, respondents could choose an answer between 'certainly yes', 'probably yes', 'probably no', and 'certainly no'. For those who admitted to not voting, the question read 'To the best of your knowledge, because you did not vote, will you have to ... ?', with the answer options kept identical.

Even though the questions were identical, there was a difference between the countries in the response categories. In Belgium and Brazil but not Australia, the survey question offered an explicit 'don't know' option, resulting in a much higher rate of respondents choosing this option in the first two countries. Consequently, we must be careful in comparing the answers from Australia with those from Belgium and Brazil.

We asked respondents about their perceptions of three possible consequences for not voting: filling out a form, going to court, and paying a fine. We start by focusing on respondents' perceived likelihood that voters must complete a form if they abstain. Figure 4 shows the distribution of responses. Recall that it is standard practice in Australia for abstainers to receive a formal notice asking them to provide a reason for failing to vote. In Belgium, given that the prosecution of non-voters is not a priority for the courts, no notifications or forms are sent. Finally, in Brazil, voters who decide not to pay the fine can justify their abstention by filling out a form at a regional electoral court, but no forms are sent automatically.

The distribution of responses in Figure 4 reflects to some extent the reality in each country, but we also find that citizens are very uncertain about the likelihood that they will have to fill out a form. We find that a large majority of Australian voters – about 69 per cent – think they probably or certainly will have to fill out a form if they abstain. In Belgium, where those who do not vote on election day are not sent a form, about 61 per cent still believe that abstainers have to fill out a form (combining 'probably' and 'certainly yes'). In Brazil, where filling out a form is a means to avoid paying a fine, about 65 per cent of respondents believe that they probably or certainly have to fill out a form. Figure 4 also indicates that about 18 per cent of voters in both Belgium and Brazil indicate that they do not know whether voters have to fill out a form if they fail to vote. In Australia, where the 'don't know' option was not explicit, only 3 per cent of voters mention not knowing.

Next, we turn to a costlier consequence for non-voting: paying a fine and here there is considerable variation in the laws and practices in the three countries. In Australia, non-voters who fail to provide a valid excuse for abstaining have to pay a A\$20 fine. As discussed in Section 2, about any excuse for not voting is considered valid, and thus very few voters in Australia pay the penalty. In Belgium, no fines have been levied in recent elections. Finally, in Brazil, one of the options for non-voters to remedy their failure of voting is to pay a small fine (less than US\$1). Paying this fine is the most common option adopted by Brazilians. Objectively, the likelihood that non-voters will have to pay a fine is higher in Brazil, followed by Australia and Belgium, in that order.

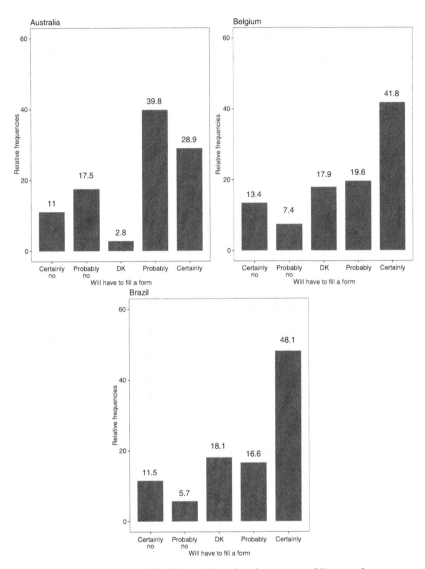

Figure 4 Perceived likelihood that abstainers must fill out a form

Note: Bars show the per cent of respondents giving a particular answer.

Figure 5 shows the distribution of responses. The results show that a substantial majority of Brazilian respondents think that they 'probably' or 'certainly' have to pay a fine if they abstain. Combining the 'certainly' and 'probably' categories, 77 per cent of Brazilians think they have to pay a fine when abstaining. Interestingly, 86 per cent of Australians also believe that they have to pay a fine for not voting. This result is surprising, given that most excuses for abstaining are acceptable in Australia, and very few are left paying a fine. Finally, about

60 per cent of respondents in Belgium believe that they have to pay a fine. Although fewer voters in Belgium believe that they will have to pay a fine for not voting, as compared to Australia and Brazil, it is remarkable that so many believe that they have to do so even though no fine for abstaining has been levied since the mid-2000s and despite the policy not to enforce compulsory voting being announced publicly. Figure 5 also shows that 8 per cent and 7 per cent of

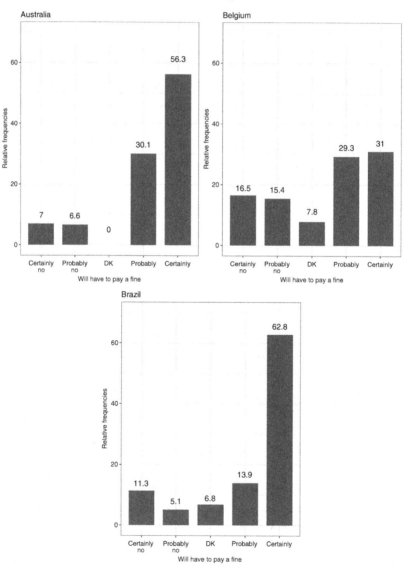

Figure 5 Perceived likelihood that abstainers must pay a fine

Note: Bars show the per cent of respondents giving a particular answer.

voters in Belgium and Brazil, respectively, do not know if they have to pay a fine for abstaining.

Finally, we turn to citizens' perceptions that abstainers must appear in court. This is the least likely consequence of abstaining in all three countries – although it is more common in Brazil, where providing an excuse for not voting to the court is one option to remedy a failure to vote. Figure 6 shows that more

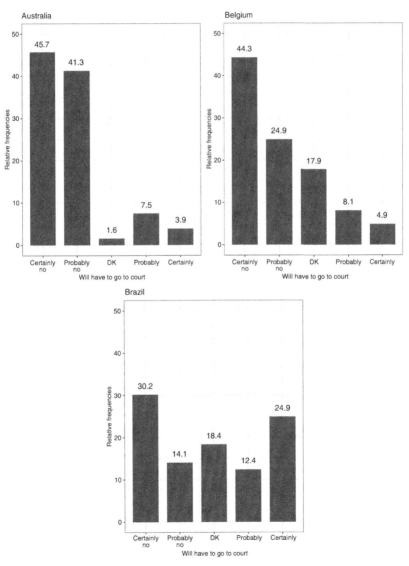

Figure 6 Perceived likelihood that abstainers must go to court

Note: Bars show the per cent of respondents giving a particular answer.

than a third of voters (37 per cent) in Brazil believe that appearing in court is probable or certain to occur when they do not vote in an election. In Australia and Belgium, significantly fewer respondents think that abstainers have to go to court. Still, about 11 per cent of Australians and 13 per cent of Belgians think so. Of the three consequences considered in our analysis, this is the one for which perceptions align most closely with reality. The proportion of voters who do not know if they have to go to court is high in both Belgium (17 per cent) and Brazil (18 per cent), however, indicating that many voters are unsure about this rare consequence.

In sum, the distributions of voters' responses to the three survey items show that differences in practices of sanctioning and the enforcement of compulsory voting are not very well reflected in what citizens perceive to be the consequences of abstaining. We observe that many voters exaggerate the consequences of not voting on election day. Specifically, many voters wrongly believe that abstention carries consequences that are not, in practice, put in place or affect large numbers of non-voters, like having to fill out a form (Belgium) or pay a fine (Australia and Belgium). Moreover, many voters simply do not know, and admit to, the consequences of failing to vote.

3.2 Political Interest and the Perceived Consequences of Abstention

Looking at citizens' perceptions about the consequences of abstention and contrasting that to the reality in the three countries suggest that many either do not know what happens when someone does not vote or hold inaccurate perceptions. The distribution of citizens' responses to the three survey items suggests that there is considerable variation in what citizens think are the consequences of abstention.

We leverage that variation to verify whether citizens who are generally more interested in politics have perceptions that better reflect reality. We centre on political interest, as a proxy for motivation, for two reasons. First, Luskin (1990) identifies political interest as one of the two main determinants, together with cognitive ability, of political sophistication. In other words, politically interested people are motivated to learn about politics and, not surprisingly, they show higher levels of information acquisition and organization. Second, political interest fosters greater electoral participation by reducing the costs associated with voting. Pattie and Johnston (1998), for example, show that voters interested in the electoral outcome were more likely to vote than those who showed less interest, presumably because it lowered the costs associated with information acquisition. Political interest, they argue, is enough for many to bear the costs of voting. In sum, motivation – as proxied by political interest – explains information acquisition and, in turn, the decision to vote by reducing the costs associated with voting.

We estimate three regression models in each country, respectively explaining respondents' perceptions about abstainers having to fill out a form, pay a fine, and go to court. We code the dependent variables to run from 0 to 1, where 0 corresponds to 'certainly no' and 1 means 'certainly yes'. We are particularly interested in the correlation between political interest and respondents' perceptions about the consequences of abstention. We therefore present the results of bivariate analyses that only focus on political interest.[7] The political interest variable ranges from 0 to 1, where 0 corresponds to 'not at all interested' and 1 'very interested' in politics.

Table 2 presents the bivariate regression estimates from regressing the respondents' perceptions that abstainers must fill out a form, pay a fine, or go to court on political interest. The first three models show the results for the perceived likelihood that non-voters have to fill out a form. The estimates indicate that in Australia and Brazil, the two countries where non-voters may have to complete a form, political interest is positively and significantly associated with perceiving the requirement to fill out a form as more likely. The size of these effects, however, is substantively very small. The perception that non-voters have to fill out a form is only seven and eight percentage points, respectively, higher among the most politically interested, as compared to the least politically interested. In Belgium – where there is no need to fill out a form – political interest does not affect such perceptions.

The next three columns in Table 2 show the association between political interest and citizens' perceived likelihood that abstainers have to pay a fine. The results indicate that in Australia, where fines are a possibility (although most excuses for abstention are accepted), the more politically interested rate the likelihood of having to pay a fine significantly higher. In Brazil, where paying a fine is the most common option for non-voters to remedy their failure to vote, there is no significant association between respondents' political interest and how likely they think that abstainers have to pay a fine. Finally, in Belgium the more politically interested are more aware of the fact that abstainers do not have to pay a fine. Announcements by public officials that abstainers would not be fined seem to have reached the most politically interested. This last finding could explain why compulsory voting exerts a stronger effect on turnout among

---

[7] In online Appendix B we show that results are similar when including standard socio-demographic controls in the models like the respondents' sex, age, level of education, and region for respondents in Belgium.

Table 2 Explaining the perceived likelihood that abstainers have to fill out a form, pay a fine or go to court – bivariate OLS regression estimates with political interest as the sole independent variable

	Have to fill out a form			Have to pay a fine			Have to go to court		
	Australia	Belgium	Brazil	Australia	Belgium	Brazil	Australia	Belgium	Brazil
Political interest	0.070*	−0.073	0.081***	0.083***	−0.115***	−0.010	0.006	−0.057*	−0.040*
	(0.028)	(0.038)	(0.015)	(0.025)	(0.035)	(0.015)	(0.022)	(0.029)	(0.017)
(Intercept)	0.602***	0.713***	0.666***	0.754***	0.673***	0.785***	0.203***	0.294***	0.491***
	(0.019)	(0.024)	(0.010)	(0.017)	(0.022)	(0.010)	(0.015)	(0.018)	(0.011)
Num.Obs.	1838	1139	5078	1836	1542	5078	1836	1406	5078
R2	0.003	0.003	0.006	0.006	0.007	0.000	0.000	0.003	0.001

Note: Estimates and standard errors (in parentheses) were obtained from OLS. Significance levels: *$p < 0.05$, **$p < 0.01$, ***$p < 0.001$.

the least interested (Söderlund et al. 2011), although many uninterested voters spoil their ballots (Slovak and Vassil 2015). Among the more politically interested, compulsory voting would not, therefore, exert much effect.

Finally, we explore the correlates of respondents' perceived likelihood that non-voters will have to go to court. This is the least likely outcome in each of the three countries and only in Brazil appearing in front of the court is a real option. Surprisingly, the results in Table 2 suggest that political interest is not significantly correlated with the perception that abstainers must appear in court in Australia. The association between political interest and the perception that abstainers must appear in court in Belgium and Brazil, for their part, is negative but substantively very weak. Although going to court is a very unlikely outcome of non-voting, especially in Australia and Belgium, the most politically interested do not appear to rate this possibility much lower than individuals who indicate that they are not very interested in politics.

Our results indicate that citizens in Australia, Belgium, and Brazil are not well informed about the legal consequences of abstaining. Many overestimate the consequences of not voting, and there are few instances where a higher level of political interest helps citizens to correct these views in a meaningful way. When it is clear whether an outcome applies to a country or not, the more politically interested appear to be more aware of this. In Australia and Brazil, where abstainers may have to fill out a form, the politically interested are more aware of this possible consequence. And in Belgium, where fines have not been levied on abstainers for some time, political interest is negatively associated with the perceived likelihood that non-voters have to pay a fine. For many other outcomes, however, there is no indication that being more politically interested affects citizens' perceptions of what happens when they abstain.

3.3 Citizens' Knowledge of Age Restrictions and Compulsory Voting Laws: The Case of Brazil

Citizens' knowledge about the consequences of non-voting in compulsory voting countries appears to be limited. As indicated in Section 1, variation in compulsory voting rules and how they are applied is not limited to differences in enforcement. Compulsory voting laws also establish criteria by which voters are required to vote. In some countries, all citizens of voting age are required to vote. In others, only those of certain ages are required to vote by law (e.g., Argentina (18–70), Brazil (18–70), Ecuador (18–65), Luxembourg (18–75) and Peru (18–70)). And in others, illiterates (e.g., Brazil and Ecuador) and Indigenous people (e.g., Brazil and Australia from 1949 to 1984) are exempt from the requirement to vote. In this subsection we are interested in the age criterion because it assigns voters to one condition (voluntary voting) or another (compulsory voting). In countries with such an institutional arrangement, the date of interest to distinguish between individuals for whom voting is compulsory and those for whom it is not is generally the election day. Those who fall within the specified age range on *that* day are required to vote by law. In Brazil, for example, younger (older) voters, even by one day, can choose to abstain without legal consequences.

Much research has shown that voters are generally ill-informed about politics (Converse 1964; Delli Carpini and Keeter 1996) – if not misinformed (Berinsky 2017; Kuklinski et al. 2001) – and things are not different concerning knowledge of compulsory voting laws (Cepaluni and Hidalgo 2016; Jaitman 2013; Turgeon and Blais 2021). In a survey conducted in 2014 with a national sample of 1,230 respondents in Brazil, Cepaluni and Hidalgo (2016) find that only 47 per cent and 34 per cent know that voting becomes compulsory at eighteen and voluntary again at seventy, respectively. Similarly, by surveying a representative sample of 500 Argentine voters aged around seventy, Jaitman (2013) reports that only 75 per cent of them are aware that voting is compulsory, although Argentina has had compulsory voting since 1912.

Neither Australia nor Belgium set age limits for compulsory voting, but Brazil does. To gain insights into the knowledge of Brazilian citizens about the criteria by which voters are required to vote, we make use of a separate survey from Brazil. This survey was conducted in late September and early October 2018, just before the first round of the Brazilian national elections. Like our main survey, this was an online survey, providing data from a sample of 8,008 voters aged eighteen to sixty-nine (i.e., the age range for which voting is compulsory). Again, respondents were not randomly selected from the Brazilian population, but the sample matches the population's main characteristics of age, sex, region, race, and social class. Respondents in this survey were randomly assigned to receive one of three different sets of questions about knowledge of compulsory voting laws in Brazil with a particular interest in how the age criterion applies. The first set of questions asked respondents if the following three statements are TRUE or FALSE: (1) All voters who are eighteen on election day are obliged to vote (TRUE); (2) All voters who are seventy on election day are *not* obliged to vote (TRUE); (3) All voters who are sixteen on election day are obliged to vote (FALSE).

We list the percentage of correct, incorrect, and don't know answers to these knowledge questions in Table 3. As shown in lines 1–3 of Table 3, nearly all respondents (about 90 per cent) correctly identified the correct statements. Overall, results indicate that most Brazilian voters are aware that voting is compulsory by law for some voters but not for others. This is reassuring and

Table 3 Knowledge about age restrictions to compulsory voting in Brazil

	% correct	% incorrect	% don't know
1. Those who are eighteen years of age on election day are obliged to vote	93.2	5.8	0.9
2. Those who are seventy years of age on election day are *not* obliged to vote	86.4	9.4	4.2
3. Those who are sixteen years of age on election day are obliged to vote	88.0	9.0	3.1
4. Those who turn eighteen this year, including those turning eighteen after election day, are obliged to vote	30.9	63.8	5.3
5. Those who turn seventy this year, including those turning seventy after election day, are *not* obliged to vote	18.1	75.6	6.3
6. Those who turn sixteen this year, including those turning sixteen after election day, are obliged to vote	84.6	10.8	4.7
7. As you may know, voting is compulsory until age seventy. Does this mean that: (a) you are still obliged to vote at seventy and no longer obliged when you reach seventy-one; or (b) you are no longer obliged to vote as soon as you reach seventy.	45.9	49.9	4.1

Note: Entries show row percentages of the distribution of answers for each knowledge item.

suggests that knowledge about this aspect of how compulsory voting is implemented in Brazil is widespread.

The second battery of questions, presented to a different group of respondents, delves deeper and asks about *how exactly* the age criterion applies. Remember that the cut point for determining whether a voter falls in the compulsory voting age range in Brazil is the voter's age on election day. Respondents in the second group were asked to indicate whether the following three statements are TRUE or FALSE: (1) All voters who turn eighteen this year, including those who turn eighteen *after* election day, are obliged to vote (FALSE); (2) All voters who turn seventy this year, including those who turn seventy *after* election day, are *not* obliged to vote (FALSE); and, (3) All voters who turn sixteen this year, including those who turn sixteen *after* election day, are obliged to vote (FALSE). As can be seen from the entries on lines 4–6 of Table 3, about a third of respondents (31 per cent) got the first item right, less than one in five (18 per cent) the second item, but the great majority of them (85 per cent) did answer the last item correctly. This second battery of questions shows that nearly all voters know that sixteen-year-olds are not required to vote by law. It also shows, however, that most voters are generally misinformed about how the age criterion applies to those who turn eighteen or seventy in an election year.

A third and last group of respondents was asked three additional questions, of which only one was related to the age criterion. The question of interest asked respondents to choose between two statements (randomly ordered):

As you may know, voting is compulsory until age seventy. Does this mean that:
a) you are still obliged to vote at seventy and no longer obliged when you reach
seventy-one
OR
b) you are no longer obliged to vote as soon as you reach seventy.

The correct answer is that you are no longer obliged to vote as soon as you reach seventy, but only 46 per cent selected that option. Some 50 per cent wrongly chose the first option, and 4 per cent responded that they did not know. This last question confirms that there is substantial confusion about how the age criterion applies to older voters.

The results are not much different when we only consider young (18–20) and old (61–69) voters, for whom the questions are most relevant. Again, large majorities of young and old voters know that voting is compulsory in Brazil between eighteen and seventy, but most are unsure about how the age criterion applies and whether voluntary voting includes voters aged seventy or not (see online Appendix C). More educated voters (i.e., those who have finished secondary education) show systematically greater knowledge (although substantially still low) of the compulsory voting laws in Brazil. The bottom line, however, is that most voters have only a very general idea of how compulsory voting laws apply in Brazil, and many are uncertain or wrong when asked about how specifically the compulsory voting criteria apply.

3.4 Summary and Implications

In compulsory voting countries, citizens entitled to vote are legally required to turn out. The ways in which countries enforce this law and how it applies, however, vary considerably. While citizens who live in a compulsory voting country are generally aware of the obligation to vote, we find that there is a great deal of uncertainty and misinformation about the implementation of the law. Many voters overstate the consequences of abstention, indicating, for example, that having to appear in court is very likely when, in fact, it rarely happens. Even those who self-report that they are very interested in politics do not appear to be much more informed than respondents who show no interest at all.

By leveraging a complementary survey from Brazil, we also showed that citizens' lack of knowledge about compulsory voting is not restricted to issues of enforcement. The second survey from Brazil shows that there is considerable confusion when it comes to the age limits that restrict compulsory voting. Most people have a general sense of the rules but lack information about how the law is applied in practice.

The analyses in this section indicate that citizens in compulsory voting countries only have a broad idea about how the system operates. This lack of information generally takes the form of citizens overestimating the costs of abstention. If citizens think the consequences of abstention are more severe than they truly are, this may affect how supportive they are of a system of compulsory voting and how much they comply with the law. In Section 4, we turn to the former question and explore public support for compulsory voting in Australia, Belgium, and Brazil.

4 Support for Compulsory Voting

Few countries rely on a system of compulsory voting and in recent decades several have shifted from compulsory to voluntary voting. Increasingly, countries where voters are compelled to turn out to vote deviate from the international norm. In the Flemish region of Belgium, where the ruling majority has voted in favour of abolishing compulsory voting for local elections, the political elites seem aware of this fact. By abolishing compulsory voting, it is argued, the organization of local elections in Flanders will fall more in line with practices elsewhere.

> In most contemporary democracies, eligible citizens are free to participate or not in the election and to cast a vote for the candidates running in the election. Flanders is lagging behind by still mandating voting and even criminalizing non-compliance with the law.
>
> Draft decree to change several decrees to strengthen local democracy, Flemish Parliament, 10 May 2021, p. 5

Therefore, countries that mandate citizens to turn out to vote are a democratic anomaly. However, how do citizens in countries that mandate voting view this rule? Arguably, whether compulsory voting can be maintained in these countries depends on how broad support is for compulsory voting. If citizens generally approve mandatory voting, they will likely comply with the rule, making it easier to sustain it. Furthermore, support for compulsory voting is a political attitude that is of interest as an indicator of political support. According to Chapman (2019: 105), citizens who indicate that they are in favour of a system of compulsory voting 'clearly express a public belief in and commitment to the value of all citizens' participation in democracy' (see also, Engelen 2007).

Despite its importance, we know little about how broad support for compulsory voting is in countries that mandate it. What we know, furthermore, comes from single-country studies. In Australia, where surveys allow tracking support for compulsory voting since the 1940s, citizens appear to be largely in favour of the rule. Surveys show that between 60 per cent and 75 per cent of Australian voters support compulsory voting (Mackerras and McAllister 1999). Section 2, however, has shown that there is considerable variation between countries in terms of the nature of compulsory voting and its enforcement. Such factors likely affect citizens' evaluations.

In this section, we examine citizens' levels of support for compulsory voting in Australia, Belgium, and Brazil. Making use of an identical question tapping support for compulsory voting, we first assess the distribution in levels of support across the three countries. We then analyse the correlates of support. Finally, we explore whether supporters of some parties are more (less) favourable.

4.1 How Popular is Compulsory Voting?

The three surveys included the following question: 'Do you think that voting at Federal elections should be compulsory, or do you think that people should only have to vote if they want to?'. The answer options were 'strongly favour people voting only if they want to', 'favour people voting only if they want to', 'favour compulsory voting' and 'strongly favour compulsory voting'.

Figure 7 presents descriptive statistics of respondents' answers. The panels in Figure 7 show substantial between-country variation in levels of support. Support is strongest in Australia, where almost three in four respondents indicate that they favour compulsory voting. More than half of the Australian respondents even have a strong preference for compulsory voting. In Belgium, public opinion is more divided. While 46 per cent of respondents favour voluntary voting, 54 per cent prefer a system of compulsory voting. A narrow majority thus supports compulsory voting. Finally, we find weak

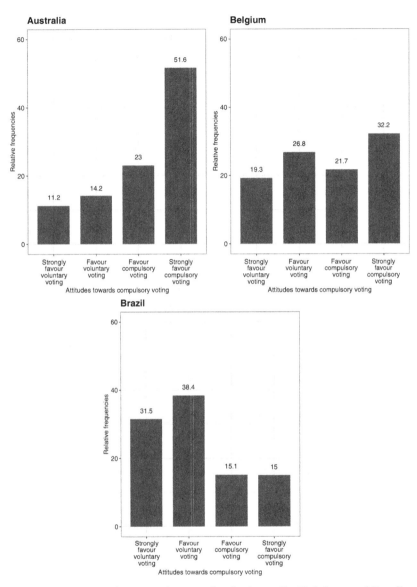

Figure 7 Support for compulsory voting in Australia, Belgium, and Brazil
Note: Bars show the per cent of respondents giving a particular answer.

support for mandatory turnout in Brazil. Among survey respondents, only 30 per cent indicated that they support compulsory voting for federal elections, while 70 per cent indicate a preference for voluntary voting.

Figure 7 indicates that there are important between-country differences in support for compulsory voting. In Belgium, public opinion is evenly balanced between opponents and supporters of compulsory voting, while the distributions are lopsided in Australia and Brazil – but in opposite directions. We conclude that compulsory voting is highly popular in Australia – where only slightly more than 10 per cent have a strong preference for a voluntary voting system – and that it is highly unpopular in Brazil. Clearly, compulsory voting is weakly institutionalized in Brazil.

4.2 Who Supports Compulsory Voting?

To explain variations in support for compulsory voting, we examine whether the coalition of citizens that supports compulsory voting in each country consists of citizens with largely similar profiles – or whether the characteristics of those who are in favour of or opposed to compulsory voting differ between countries as well.

We focus on three socio-demographic characteristics: respondents' sex, age, and level of education. Age and education are the two most studied and most powerful socio-demographic correlates of turnout (Blais and Anduiza 2013; Smets and van Ham 2013). As for sex, it is associated with citizens' level of information and interest in politics (Dassonneville and Kostelka 2021; Dassonneville and McAllister 2018; Jerit and Barabas 2017), for which there is a relatively large gender gap, and which are bound to shape citizens' views about compulsory voting. We estimate the effect of being a woman – using men as the reference category. We include age as a continuous variable (divided by 10 so the coefficient captures the effect of being ten years older), and evaluate the effect of education by distinguishing between respondents who hold a higher education degree against those with lower educational attainment. Finally, in Belgium we add a control to distinguish between respondents from Wallonia and Flanders (the reference). We study the association between these socio-demographic variables and support for compulsory voting employing country-specific models that rely on OLS estimation, in which 'Support for compulsory voting' (cf. Figure 7) is the dependent variable.[8] This variable is coded to run from 0 to 1, where 0 signifies a strong preference for voluntary voting and 1 signifies a strong preference for compulsory voting.

Table 4 presents the results of these regression models. Note, first, that support for compulsory voting is significantly higher among Walloon respondents than among the Flemish – which highlights the importance of accounting for the differences between the two regions in our estimations. Of the three socio-demographic variables that are included in each model, only one has

---

[8] When estimating ordered logit models instead, the results are substantively similar (see online Appendix D).

Table 4 Explaining support for compulsory voting, socio-demographics

	Australia	**Belgium**	**Brazil**
Female	0.038*	0.040*	0.026**
	(0.015)	(0.018)	(0.009)
Age (x 10 years)	0.010*	0.002	−0.053***
	(0.004)	(0.005)	(0.003)
Higher education	0.092***	0.139***	−0.020*
	(0.018)	(0.019)	(0.009)
Walloon region		0.050***	
		(0.019)	
Intercept	0.624***	0.455***	0.571***
	(0.025)	(0.034)	(0.015)
Num.Obs.	1994	1727	5078
R2	0.018	0.038	0.054

Note: Estimates and standard errors (in parentheses) from OLS models are shown. Significance levels: $*p < 0.05$, $**p < 0.01$, $***p < 0.001$.

a consistent effect across the three countries: sex. In all countries females are more supportive of compulsory voting than male respondents. This effect is significant in every country, though the substantive difference is modest. More specifically, the coefficients vary between 0.03 and 0.04, implying that females' support for compulsory voting is 3 to 4 percentage points higher than males'.

Turning to the other socio-demographic variables, the association between age and support for compulsory voting differs in the three countries. In Australia, there is a weak positive association between age and support for compulsory voting, suggesting that older citizens are more in favour of compulsory voting. This effect is substantively very small, however, with support for compulsory voting increasing by one percentage point, on average, as respondents' age increases by ten years. The connection between age and support for compulsory voting has the opposite sign in Brazil, suggesting that older Brazilians are less supportive of compulsory voting. The effect of age in Brazil is substantial: the coefficient on the effect of age in Table 4 suggests that for each ten years increase in age, support for compulsory voting decreases by 5 percentage points. In Belgium, the association between age and support for compulsory voting is null.

Finally, we find relevant country differences concerning education and support for compulsory voting. Citizens with a higher education degree are more supportive of compulsory voting in Australia and Belgium. In both cases, the effect is significant and substantively important. In Australia, those with a higher education degree are 9 percentage points more in favour of compulsory voting than those without higher education. In Belgium, the contrast is larger, with an estimated 14 percentage points difference. In Brazil, the association between education and support for compulsory voting is not only substantially weaker but the direction of the effect is negative. In Brazil, those with a higher education degree are somewhat *less* supportive of compulsory voting. The implication is that the better educated are more supportive of compulsory voting where it is an accepted norm, in Australia and Belgium, while they are more strongly opposed where it is contested.

Table 4 suggests that having information on individuals' socio-demographic characteristics is useful for predicting their level of support for compulsory voting. The predictions that one would make, however, differ between countries. Most importantly, while a higher level of education is associated with more support for compulsory voting in Australia and Belgium, the opposite holds in Brazil. In the latter country, there are also indications that older citizens are less in favour of mandatory turnout while age seems mostly unrelated to support for compulsory voting in Australia and Belgium.

The differences in the socio-demographic profiles of those who support compulsory voting in each of the three countries are further illustrated in Figures 8, 9, and 10. These figures show the predicted level of support for compulsory voting (on a scale from 0 to 1), by respondents' sex (Figure 8), age (Figure 9), and level of education (Figure 10) – in each of the three countries – based on the estimates from Table 4. These figures illustrate (1) the differences in *levels* of support for compulsory voting and (2) the contrasts in the *associations* between specific socio-demographic variables and compulsory voting between countries – with opposite effects for age and education in Brazil than what holds for the other two countries.

Our results show substantial differences between the countries in the socio-demographic correlates of support for compulsory voting. However, the analyses also show that the combined explanatory power of the core socio-demographic variables of sex, age, and education is limited. The R^2 statistics in Table 4 indicate that the three socio-demographic variables explain between 2 per cent (in Australia) and 5 per cent (in Brazil) of the variation in support for compulsory voting. To improve our understanding of the sources of support for compulsory voting in each country, we complement the socio-demographic model and account for political interest. Political interest is measured through a four-point survey item in each of the three surveys, allowing respondents to indicate to what extent they are interested in politics. We rescaled this variable so 0 corresponds to the lowest level of interest in politics and 1 corresponds to the highest interest level.

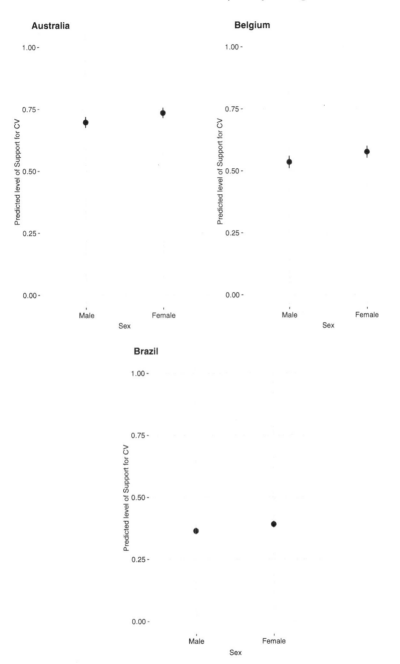

Figure 8 Predicted level of support for compulsory voting by country and citizens' sex

Note: Estimates show predicted level of support for compulsory voting in each country. Predictions are based on OLS estimations shown in Table 4.

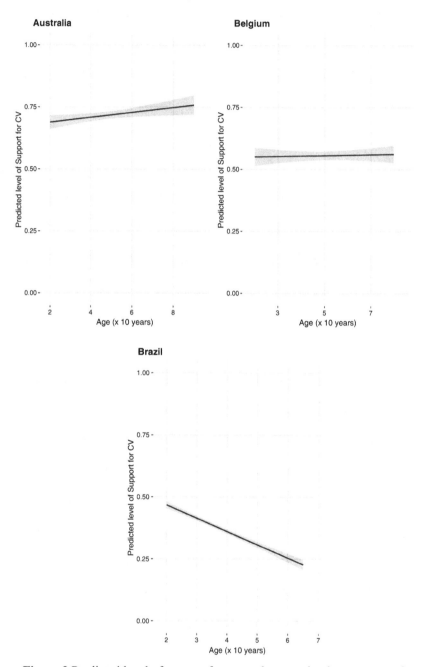

Figure 9 Predicted level of support for compulsory voting by country and citizens' age

Note: Estimates show predicted level of support for compulsory voting in each country. Predictions are based on OLS estimations shown in Table 4.

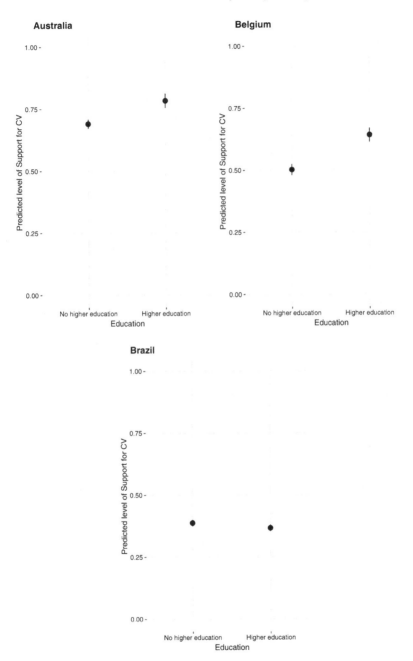

Figure 10 Predicted level of support for compulsory voting by country and citizens' level of education

Note: Estimates show predicted level of support for compulsory voting in each country. Predictions are based on OLS estimations shown in Table 4.

Figure 11 visualizes the results of the regression models that estimate the association between political interest and support for compulsory voting while controlling for respondents' socio-demographic characteristics. We plot the coefficients of the different variables by country, with 90 per cent (thick line) and 95 per cent (thin line) confidence intervals. The estimates show that in each of the three countries the association between political interest and support for compulsory voting is positive, statistically significant, and substantively strong. Citizens who have a higher level of interest in politics are consistently more supportive of compulsory voting. In each of the three countries, furthermore, the coefficient on political interest is by far the strongest predictor of compulsory voting – much stronger than respondents' sex, age, or level of education. These findings are consistent with the idea that '[t]hose who like politics are more likely to think that elections are important' and, consequently, to construe of participation as a moral obligation (Blais and Daoust 2021: 47).

The association between political interest and support for compulsory voting is substantial, but there are noteworthy differences between countries. The association is weakest in Brazil. The coefficient of political interest in Brazil is 0.17, implying that respondents with the highest level of interest in politics (value of 1 on political interest) have a 17 percentage points higher level of support for compulsory voting than the least politically interested (value of 0 on political interest). In Australia and in Belgium, the connection between political interest and support for mandatory voting is stronger, with coefficients of .31 and .38 respectively. Clearly, support for a system of compulsory voting is higher among citizens who are more interested in politics in general. This holds in Brazil, but especially in Australia and Belgium.

Finally, we explore whether there are systematic partisan differences in support for compulsory voting. A common narrative in the scholarly literature (Ferwerda 2014; Fowler 2013; Miller and Dassonneville 2016) and in the public discourse is that centre-left parties benefit from compulsory voting. In Section 6, we put this narrative to test by examining whether supporters of certain parties are more or less likely to turn out to vote if compulsory voting was abolished in Australia, Belgium, or Brazil. Regardless of whether there is evidence to support the view that centre-left parties benefit electorally from compulsory voting rules, the positions that parties take in debates about the possibility to abolish compulsory voting suggest that left-wing parties tend to be more supportive of mandating turnout than parties on the right of the ideological spectrum.

Australia provides an apt example of the importance of elite positions on compulsory voting. Jackman (1999: 31) refers to the results of a 1996 candidate survey that show that politicians of the Australian Labor Party are almost

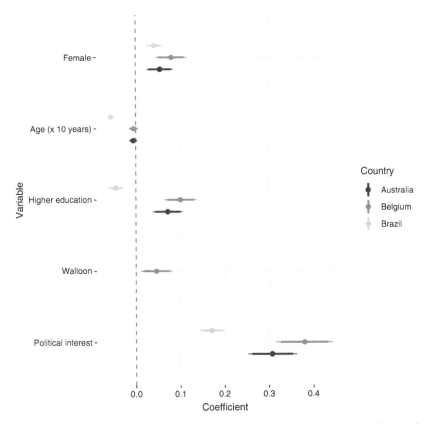

Figure 11 Explaining support for compulsory voting, socio-demographics, and political interest

Note: OLS estimates of three country-specific models predicting support for compulsory voting. 95 per cent (thin lines) and 90 per cent (thick lines) confidence intervals are added. Female is coded 1 if the respondent is female and 0 otherwise, Age is a respondent's age divided by 10, Higher education is coded 1 if the respondent has a higher education degree and 0 otherwise, Walloon is coded 1 for respondents in the Walloon sample of the Belgian survey data and 0 for respondents from the Flemish sample. Political interest is coded to range between 0 (= not at all interested) and 1 (= very interested).

unanimous in rejecting the possibility of abolishing compulsory voting (97 per cent took this position) while only 40 per cent of the right-wing Coalition's candidates took the same position. In recent years, however, parties' positions have seemingly become more consensual. Another example is Belgium, where there is a debate on the question of whether compulsory voting should be maintained. Here, it is parties that are positioned on the centre-right that favour abolishing compulsory voting. As Hooghe and Deschouwer (2011) indicate, proposals to switch to a system of voluntary voting are usually made by the liberal parties and vetoed by the Francophone socialists. And in 2021, it was the Flemish liberals who convinced their centre-right coalition partners in the Flemish government to abolish compulsory voting for municipal and provincial elections. In Brazil, there are few partisan differences on the issue of compulsory voting. According to Power (2000: 28), 'elite views ... appear to be deeply personal and do not appear to overlap with any obvious cleavage within the Brazilian political class.' The lack of a clear left-right ideological division on compulsory voting was also visible in 2015, when the right-wing party Democrats proposed an amendment to the Constitution intending to abolish mandatory voting. The proposal received support from left-wing parties (PPS and PV), while the centrist PMDB allowed their MPs a free vote on the proposal. Ultimately, the proposal was rejected by a large majority of votes coming from twenty-one different parties from both left and right (Agência Câmara 2015).

When there are differences in the positions that parties take, voters who support parties that favour a shift to voluntary voting should be less supportive of mandatory voting when compared to those who support other parties. That might be so because the party's position on compulsory voting shapes voters' choices (Kropko and Banda 2018), or because voters adjust their opinions to match those of their preferred party (Broockman and Butler 2017). To verify whether the positions of the voters of different parties broadly match the positions that parties take in debates about compulsory voting, we add to the models variables for the party (or party of the candidate) that a respondent voted for in the elections under study.

Given that the number of party options is large, especially in Belgium and Brazil, we focus on those parties that gained the support of at least 3 per cent of the respondents in a survey. To ease the interpretation of the partisan differences, and because the Belgian partisan space essentially consists of two different party systems – one with Dutch-speaking parties in Flanders and another with French-speaking parties in Wallonia (Brack and Pilet 2010) – we present separate analyses for the Flemish and Walloon subsamples in Belgium.

We summarize the results in Figure 12, by showing the predicted levels of support for compulsory voting on a scale from 0 to 1 by respondents' reported vote choice. These estimates are based on a fully specified model, holding constant respondents' socio-demographic characteristics and their level of political interest. As a point of comparison, the graphs in Figure 12 also show the average level of support for compulsory voting for the whole sample with vertical dashed lines. Figure 12 shows that in Australia partisan differences are very limited. The voters

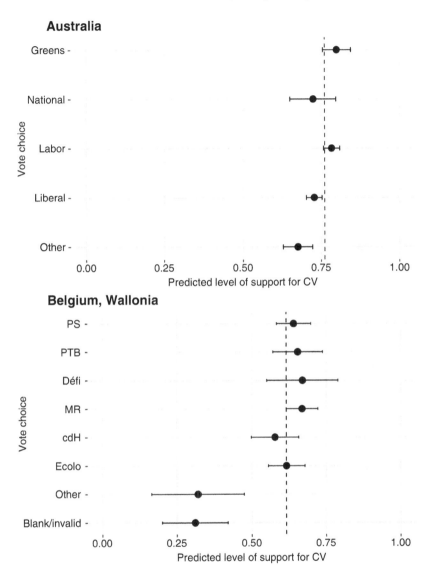

Figure 12a Partisan differences in support for compulsory voting
Note: Predicted level of support for compulsory voting with 95 per cent confidence intervals, by reported vote choice. Models include controls for respondents' socio-demographic characteristics and political interest.

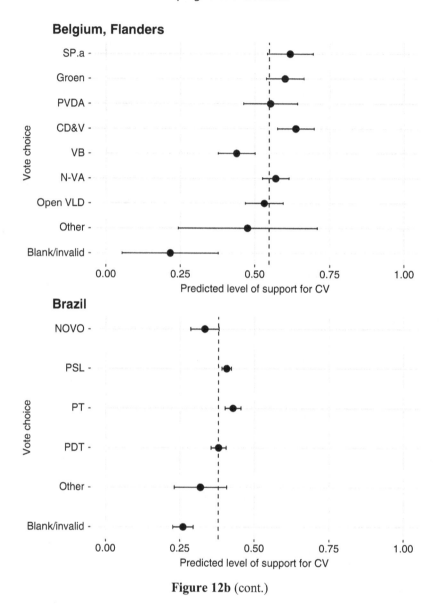

Figure 12b (cont.)

of all parties strongly support a system of compulsory voting. The only two groups for which levels of support are significantly different from the average are Liberal Party voters and those voting for other parties. In both cases, their support for compulsory voting is slightly lower than average.

Similarly, partisan differences are muted in Belgium. In the Flemish subsample, three groups stand out. First, those who indicated that they voted for the Christian-Democratic party CD&V in the 2019 federal elections are significantly more in favour of compulsory voting. However, their level of support for mandatory voting is very similar to that of supporters of Social-Democratic (SP.a) and Green (Groen) party. The only partisan group that is significantly less supportive of compulsory voting is the electorate of the extreme-right party Vlaams Belang (VB). Finally, those casting a blank or an invalid vote are significantly less supportive of compulsory voting. Partisan differences are even more limited in the Walloon subsample. Somewhat surprisingly, those who voted for the Liberal Party (MR) are among the most supportive of a system of compulsory voting, though differences with the other partisan groups are very small. The only groups that have a different level of support for compulsory voting in Wallonia are those voting for other minor parties and those casting a blank or invalid vote. Both groups are clearly less in favour of compulsory voting.

Finally, the confidence intervals in the bottom graph in Figure 12 are substantially smaller than those for the other graphs, but that reflects the larger sample size for the Brazilian survey. Levels of support for compulsory voting differ only marginally between voters of different parties. The group that is most supportive of compulsory voting consists of those who voted for Fernando Haddad – the candidate of the Worker's Party (PT) – in the 2018 presidential elections. But those who voted for the right-wing candidate Jair Bolsonaro (PSL) also appear to be more supportive of compulsory voting than the average voter. The only voters who hold views about compulsory voting that are clearly distinct from the average are those who cast a blank or invalid vote.

Overall, our analyses of partisan differences in support for compulsory voting show little evidence of party-based polarization. The predicted levels of support of voters from different parties (or candidates) cluster around the average level of support in each setting. In Australia, voters of all parties are very supportive of compulsory voting, while in Brazil supporters of all parties hold more negative views. The only groups that stand out are those supporting minor parties, those who vote for the extreme-right (in the Flemish context) and – unsurprisingly – those who end up casting a blank or invalid vote.

4.3 Summary and Implications

We know little about how citizens view compulsory voting in countries that mandate citizens to participate in elections. By surveying citizens in Australia, Belgium, and Brazil and using a question with the exact same wording across the three countries, we can compare levels of support between countries. Our results show that citizens' support for compulsory voting differs markedly between countries. Australians are strongly in favour of compulsory voting, Belgians are divided, and Brazilians are strongly opposed. This ordering of levels of support in the three countries corresponds to the extent to which citizens comply with compulsory voting. That is, official turnout data show that turnout rates are highest in Australia, followed by Belgium and Brazil, in that order.

In terms of the characteristics of those who are in favour of compulsory voting, we find that women and those who are more interested in politics show higher levels of support for compulsory voting. The profile of those supporting compulsory voting differs, however, when we consider citizens' age and their level of education. First, while there are hardly any age differences in support for compulsory voting in Australia and Belgium, in Brazil, older voters are significantly less in favour of mandatory voting. The contrast between Australia and Belgium, on the one hand, and Brazil, on the other, is most pronounced when assessing the educational profile of those supporting compulsory voting. In the former two countries, higher education is positively associated with support for compulsory voting, while the opposite holds in Brazil. Not only is citizens' support for compulsory voting lower in Brazil, support for the institution, contrary to Australia and Belgium, is slightly higher among younger and lower-educated voters.

Finally, our analyses of partisan differences in citizens' levels of support for compulsory voting show that these are very limited. Except for those voting for fringe parties or not casting a valid vote at all, different partisan groups have similar levels of support for compulsory voting. The lack of substantial partisan differences likely reflects the lack of debate at the elite level about whether or not to maintain compulsory voting in the three countries. In Australia, while the Liberal Party has argued against mandatory voting in the past, recent party leaders have expressed support for the measure. In Belgium, even though the Liberal party occasionally starts a debate about the question (and did so in the Flemish parliament following the 2019 elections), compulsory voting is not a campaign issue. Finally, in Brazil, even though abolishing compulsory voting has been debated in Parliament, elite-level positions on the issue appear to be mainly personal.

5 Compulsory Voting Works: It Increases Turnout

The most direct objective of compulsory voting is to increase turnout by requiring everyone to vote. Theoretically, therefore, in countries that mandate voting turnout should be 100 per cent. In practice, some people may not be able to vote, because of sickness for instance. Furthermore, some may not want to vote, and the state may not be able to force everyone to vote. There are thus practical constraints that make it impossible to attain full participation.

Even though compulsory voting countries cannot attain full participation, obliging citizens to turn out to vote should still have a big positive impact on electoral participation. Is it the case? The simple answer is: yes. Many studies have examined the correlates of voter turnout, including the role of institutional variables like compulsory voting. Based on a meta-analysis of existing studies that have examined the predictors of aggregate-level turnout, Stockemer (2017: 703) concludes that 'In the over 130 models in which [compulsory voting] is used, it is positively and statistically significantly related to turnout in all but four cases.' This finding is consistent with previous reviews of the literature (Blais 2006; Geys 2006). There is a scientific consensus that in mandatory voting countries electoral participation is significantly higher than in voluntary voting countries.

Compulsory voting fosters participation, but how big is the impact of compulsory voting on turnout? According to Blais (2006: 112–3) the estimated effect that is reported in cross-national studies is 'almost always around 10 to 15 [percentage] points.' Given that turnout in the absence of compulsory voting is typically around 67 per cent (see Kostelka, Singh and Blais 2021: figure 6), this suggests that turnout is about 80 per cent when it is compulsory, a relative increase of 19 per cent. In other words, about 39 per cent of those who would not vote in the absence of compulsory voting cast a vote when they are obliged to. Compulsory voting is not fully successful and does not ensure full participation, but it does work.

Another way to assess the impact of compulsory voting rules on turnout levels is to examine what happens when mandatory turnout is abolished. The trends in turnout in countries that switched to a voluntary voting system further confirm the strong effects of this institution. In the Netherlands, the abolition of compulsory voting in 1970 resulted in a 15 percentage points decline in turnout (Hirczy 1994). In Venezuela, which abolished compulsory voting in 1993, turnout declined even more and dropped about 20 percentage points following the switch to voluntary voting (Carey and Horiuchi 2017).

While the effects of compulsory voting on electoral participation are well-established, the reasons *why* compulsory voting rules have such strong effects on turnout are less well known. In this section, we seek to gain more insights into the reasons for the effectiveness of compulsory voting. As with the previous sections, we shed light on this question by analysing citizens' attitudes and behaviour – as captured by the surveys in Australia, Belgium, and Brazil.

5.1 Why Does Compulsory Voting Work?

In countries that mandate turnout, levels of electoral participation are substantially higher than in voluntary voting countries. Even though this is hardly surprising, scholars have been puzzled by the size of the impact that compulsory voting seems to have on turnout. Lijphart (1997: 9) states that scholars have been 'surprised by the strong effect of the obligation to vote, especially in view of the generally low penalties for noncompliance and generally lax enforcement.' Two broad sets of explanations have been provided to explain the strong effects of mandatory voting. Some have argued that compulsory voting rules are effective because they serve to signal to voters that it is their duty to vote (Engelen 2007) and that electoral participation represents 'good behaviour' (Chapman 2019). This supposes that the effects of compulsory voting are largely symbolic. Others argue that enforcement is crucial and contend that penalties for not voting are key (Panagopoulos 2008; Singh 2015).

The issue, therefore, is the role of sanctions and their enforcement in compulsory voting systems. As indicated in Section 2, there is much variation in compulsory voting rules and in their application. There are countries where the constitution or the law stipulates that voting is an obligation but there are no sanctions for abstention. In other settings, there are sanctions, but these sanctions are very weak or rarely enforced. And in other countries sanctions are more consequential or strictly enforced. What do we know about the importance of the presence of sanctions and the degree of enforcement of these sanctions for turnout?

The literature on the role of sanctions and their enforcement is scarce. The available evidence, however, strongly suggests that sanctions and enforcement matter. Fornos, Power and Garand (2004), who study turnout in Latin America, construct a 4-point compulsory voting scale that goes from 0 for countries with voluntary voting to 3 for those with compulsory voting and legal sanctions that are enforced in practice. Using this measure, they find that turnout increases by 5 points for every one-point increase on the compulsory voting scale. Based on this work, however, we cannot conclude whether the effect is linear or not. It might be that weak sanctions suffice to mobilize citizens, or that turnout is only high when sanctions are severe and enforced.

We gain more nuanced insights into the importance of sanctions and enforcement from the work of Birch (2009: 93–4) and Panagopoulos (2008). Both scholars report that when compulsory voting is unenforced or weakly enforced, levels of turnout are not higher than in voluntary voting systems. Such observations suggest that the presence of real and serious sanctions is a necessary condition for compulsory voting to work. That conclusion has recently been challenged by Kostelka, Singh and Blais (2021). They also find that the impact of compulsory voting depends on the presence of sanctions and the state's capacity to implement these sanctions, but they indicate that compulsory voting with no real sanction still has a meaningful (though smaller) impact on turnout, of 7 to 10 percentage points.

5.2 Does Compulsory Voting Work in Australia, Belgium, and Brazil?

How successful is compulsory voting – in terms of its capacity to increase turnout – in each of the three countries on which we focus in this Element? And how important are sanctions and their perceived enforcement?

A first observation is that turnout is very high in each of the three countries. The percentage of registered voters who cast a vote is around 90 per cent in Australia and Belgium. It is somewhat lower, but still around 80 per cent, in post-1985 elections in Brazil. In each of the three countries, turnout is much higher than what is usually observed in countries with voluntary voting.

Even though turnout is systematically high in each of the three countries, it is not a complete success. About 10 per cent of citizens do not cast a vote in recent elections in Australia and Belgium and about 20 per cent do not turn out to vote in Brazil. The difference in turnout rates between Australia and Belgium, on the one hand, and Brazil on the other, raises the question about whether the lower turnout observed in Brazil is due to weaker sanctions (or enforcement) or to the fact that compulsory voting does not apply to everyone (those under eighteen and over seventy, illiterates, as well as Indigenous people, are exempt). Alternatively, it could be the case that the 'normal' turnout (under voluntary voting) is lower in Brazil than it is in Australia and Belgium because the country is poorer, with more illiterates, and is a non-established democracy – which are all factors that are associated with lower turnout (Blais and Dobrzynska 1998).

A straightforward way to ascertain the impact of compulsory voting is to ask those who voted, under mandatory voting rules, whether they would have voted in the absence of a CV or not. Our survey data included such a question for each of the three countries. We asked respondents 'How likely is it that you would have voted in the election if voting had not been compulsory, would you say you . . . ?' Respondents could indicate that they 'definitely would have voted', 'probably would have voted', 'might or might not have voted', 'probably would not have voted', and 'definitely would not have voted'.

There are, of course, limitations in the conclusions that can be drawn when survey respondents are asked about their future behaviour, for example, whether they would vote if the electoral system changed from compulsory to voluntary voting. It is argued that individuals find it difficult to forecast changes in their behaviour under counterfactual scenarios. We address this criticism in two ways. First, numerous studies find that under certain conditions, an attitude is a strong predictor of future behaviour. If the attitude is grounded in current or past behaviour then it will be an accurate predictor of future behaviour (for a review, see Ajzen 2018). Similarly, the prediction is more reliable if the attitude displays long-term stability and is reported frequently or reflected in recurrent behaviour (Glasman and Albarracín 2006). Compulsory voting is a regular and familial behaviour. We therefore believe that our survey questions about future behaviour are accurate predictions of what would occur in practice.

The second way in which we can assess the accuracy of future predictions of behaviour is to examine real-world examples. First, we consider what happened when the Netherlands moved from compulsory to voluntary voting in 1970. The relative decline in turnout in the Netherlands between 1967 (the last election conducted under compulsory voting) and the two elections immediately after, in 1971 and 1972, was 14.6 percent (Irwin 1974). If we compare this with a hypothetical survey question (in this case from the 2019 election survey from Belgium) about whether the respondents would vote if the system moved from compulsory to voluntary voting, we find that there would be a decline in turnout of 16 percent – a similar drop in turnout as occurred in the Netherlands between 1967 and 1972.[9] While this comparison involves different countries at different time periods, it provides strong suggestive evidence that in our case future predictions of mass behaviour are likely to be accurate.

In addition, we can leverage the fact that voting is only compulsory for certain age groups in Brazil to verify whether the hypothetical turnout rate under voluntary voting among those who fall just short of reaching the age at which voting is no longer compulsory resembles actual turnout rates of those who have passed the age limit. We make use of the 2018 Brazil Election Study (BES), conducted by the Center for Studies on Public Opinion.[10] Respondents in the 2018 BES were asked 'In this year's elections, if voting were NOT mandatory, would you have gone to vote?' Answer options include yes, no and it depends. Given the small number of respondents choosing the last option, we focus on the per cent of respondents indicating yes or no. Of all respondents in this survey aged between sixty-five and sixty-nine – an age group closer to the voluntary voting age threshold – 48 per cent indicate that they would not vote under voluntary voting rules. In comparison, according to official data from the Superior Electoral Court (2023), 45 per cent of Brazilians between seventy and

---

[9] In the 1967, 1971, and 1974 Dutch legislative elections turnout was 94.9 per cent, 79.1 per cent, and 82.9 per cent, respectively. The average turnout in the 1971 and 1972 elections was 81.0 per cent, or a relative decline of 14.6 per cent compared to 1967.

[10] The data for this study can be accessed here www.cesop.unicamp.br/eng/eseb/ondas/11.

seventy-four, which is the age group that has just reached the age at which they are no longer mandated to vote, abstained from voting in the first round of the 2018 elections. The hypothetical turnout rate of those falling just below the voluntary voting age threshold thus approximates the actual turnout rate of those having just cleared that threshold. While only suggestive, these analyses give further validity to the survey item used in this Element.

Figure 13 presents the distribution of answers to the question asking respondents to indicate their behaviour under the hypothetical scenario of voluntary voting. The percentage of those who answered that they definitely or probably would not have voted is about 10 per cent in Australia, 16 per cent in Belgium, and 25 per cent in Brazil. Taken at face value, these numbers suggest that the impact of compulsory voting on turnout is about 9 percentage points in Australia, 14 points in Belgium, and 20 points in Brazil.[11] These estimates are in line with the estimated effects of compulsory voting with enforced sanctions, as reported in studies that have analysed within-country change over time (Carey and Horiuchi 2017; Hirczy 1994; Kostelka, Singh, and Blais 2021) or cross-national variation in turnout (Blais and Dobrzynska 1998).

Figure 13 suggests that compulsory voting has the biggest effect in Brazil and the smallest effect in Australia. We should note, however, that the values reported in Figure 13 do not take the indirect effects of compulsory voting into account (Singh 2021). There is evidence that the presence of compulsory voting fosters citizens' sense of civic duty (Feitosa, Blais, and Dassonneville 2020), leading more people in compulsory-voting countries to accept the view that they have a moral obligation to vote. This indirect effect is likely larger in Australia, where support for compulsory voting is high, and smaller in Brazil, where the legitimacy of compulsory voting is weak (see Section 4). Potentially, hence, the mobilizing effects of compulsory voting are somewhat larger than what the data in Figure 13 suggest.

5.3 Who is Affected by Compulsory Voting?

Having shown that compulsory voting in Australia, Belgium, and Brazil is effective in fostering turnout, we exploit our individual-level survey data to shed light on which groups are most affected by it. Who are those people who vote under compulsory voting and who report that they would abstain if they were not obliged to vote? As a first step, we focus on the socio-demographic

---

[11] That is, 10 per cent of a 'typical' turnout rate of 90 per cent in Australia, 16 per cent of a 'typical' turnout rate of 90 per cent in Belgium and 25 per cent of a 'typical' turnout rate of 80 per cent in Brazil.

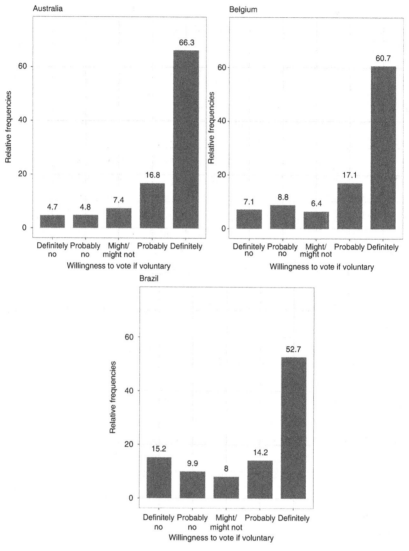

Figure 13 Intention to vote if no compulsory voting

Note: Bars show the per cent of respondents giving a particular answer. Only respondents who indicated they voted are included in the figure.

characteristics of voters, in this case the respondents' sex, age, and level of education. We include indicators for each of these three characteristics as independent variables in country-specific models estimated by OLS that seek to explain voters' reported intention to abstain from voting in a voluntary voting context. We again rescale the age variable so a one-unit increase corresponds to a respondent being ten years older. As previously, for Belgium we additionally include a control for region. We scaled the dependent variable so it captures abstention and varies between 0 for individuals who indicate they would definitely vote and 1 for respondents saying they definitely would not vote. Finally, it is important to note that these analyses only include respondents who reported to have voted in the last election, i.e., under compulsory voting rules.

Figure 14 shows the results of these analyses, by means of a coefficient plot that presents the estimated effects of the socio-demographic variables on respondents' intention to abstain under voluntary voting. The results show that in each of the three countries, females and the less educated are more prone to say that they would abstain if voting was voluntary. The implication of this finding is that these groups – women and the lower educated – are more strongly affected by the presence of compulsory voting and that turnout would be particularly lower in these groups under voluntary voting rules. While the effect of respondents' sex is fairly consistent across countries, there is more variation in the effect of education. The mobilizing effect of compulsory voting among the lower educated seems to be the largest in Belgium and the smallest in Australia. Even so, in each of the three countries we see that the higher educated are significantly less likely to say they would abstain from voting if it were no longer compulsory. The impact of age, in contrast, is more ambiguous. In Australia, younger respondents are more inclined to indicate that they would abstain, but the opposite is true in Brazil. In Belgium, finally, there is no significant association between age and voters' intention to abstain under voluntary voting.

The results in Figure 14 suggest that compulsory voting contributes to lessening unequal participation. Females and the lower educated seem to be more affected by the presence of compulsory voting. By mandating voting, hence both the gender gap (Dassonneville and Kostelka 2021) and the education gap in participation (Gallego 2010) can be reduced. Furthermore, compulsory voting also seems to weaken the age gap in Australia but not in Belgium and Brazil.

Compulsory voting not only has heterogeneous effects based on citizens' socio-demographic characteristics, but it also has differential effects depending on citizens' level of interest in politics. Still using voters' reported likelihood of abstention under voluntary voting as a dependent variable, our results suggest that the impact of compulsory voting is substantially larger among those with little interest in politics. We find that those who are not interested in politics are much more likely to say that they would abstain if there was no legal obligation. Figure 15 visualizes this effect by focusing on voters' predicted intention to abstain (from 0 = definitely vote to 1 = definitely abstain), based on models that account for the socio-demographic variables shown in Figure 14 (coefficients

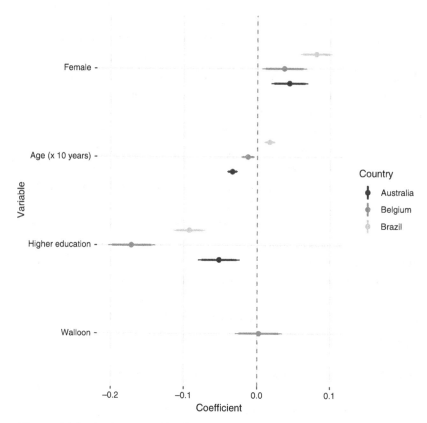

Figure 14 Socio-demographic characteristics and intention to abstain under voluntary voting

Note: OLS estimates of three country-specific models explaining intention to abstain if voting were voluntary. Spikes indicate 90 per cent (thick lines) and 95 per cent (thin lines) confidence intervals. Female is coded 1 if the respondent is female and 0 otherwise, Age is a respondent's age divided by 10, Higher education is coded 1 if the respondent has a higher education degree and 0 otherwise, Walloon is coded 1 for respondents in the Walloon sample of the Belgian survey data and 0 for respondents from the Flemish sample. Detailed estimates can be found in online Appendix E.

can be consulted in online Appendix E). Figure 15 shows how sizeable the role of political interest is. In Brazil 60 per cent of those with no interest in politics (score 0 on the 0 to 1 scale) indicate they would not vote under voluntary voting, compared with 8 per cent among those who express great interest (score of 1). The equivalent figures are 42 per cent and 0 per cent in Australia and 55 per cent and 0 per cent in Belgium. These are big effects: if Australia, Belgium, or Brazil switched to a system of voluntary voting, the least politically interested would abstain in large numbers.

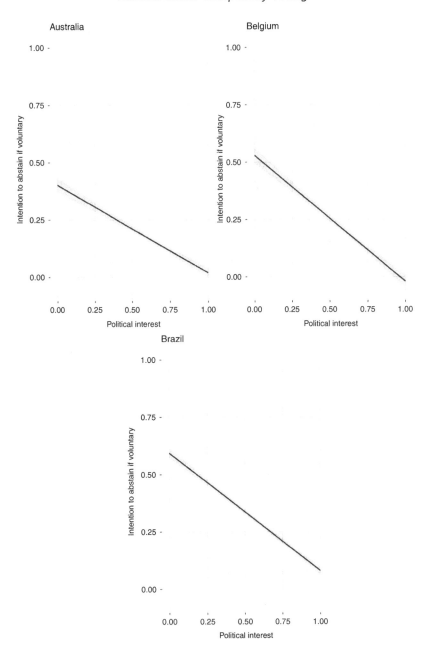

Figure 15 Predicted intention to abstain under voluntary voting, by level of interest in politics

Note: OLS estimates of three country-specific models explaining intention to abstain if voting is voluntary. The shaded area shows 95 per cent confidence intervals. Detailed estimates can be found in online Appendix E.

5.4 How Important are Sanctions in Australia, Belgium, and Brazil?

Our results so far show that compulsory voting in Australia, Belgium, and Brazil has a strong mobilizing effect. Based on respondents' intended behaviour under voluntary voting, we estimate that turnout levels would drop between 10 and 20 percentage points if these countries switched to a voluntary voting system, and the decline would be particularly noteworthy among women, the lower educated and those who are not interested in politics. The final question to address concerns the role of sanctions and enforcement in the process. We find that turnout would be substantially lower if the three countries did not mandate voting. But do we also have indications that compulsory voting is effective only (or mostly) because citizens want to avoid sanctions for abstention?

To analyse the role of sanctions and their enforcement, it is important to keep in mind that what matters is not the objective reality (i.e., the amount of fine that the law stipulates) but citizens' perceptions of these sanctions and their enforcement. Ultimately, it is these perceptions about the consequences of not turning out to vote that drive people's decision whether to vote or not. As shown in Section 3, there is much misinformation about what compulsory voting entails in each country. To know whether citizens turn out to vote to avoid the costs of abstention, it is hence crucial to consider people's subjective perceptions about the probability that they would have to fill out a form, go to court, and pay a fine if they do not vote.

To evaluate whether sanctions are key to explaining the high levels of turnout, we test a simple hypothesis: the greater the perceived sanction for abstention, the greater the propensity to vote. We are interested in those who would abstain if voting were voluntary and who ponder whether to vote or not under compulsory voting. Theoretically, if the person is convinced that there would be no consequence to abstaining, there is no additional reason to vote. If on the contrary the person is certain that they will have to fill out a form, go to court, and pay a fine, then there are strong incentives to obey the law.

In Sections 5.2 and 5.3, we focused only on those who turned out to vote and the correlates of their likelihood to abstain if voting were voluntary. For our analysis of turnout, we return to the full samples. Our dependent variable is whether the person voted or not in the election. Reported turnout among survey respondents is 93 per cent in Australia, 92 per cent in Belgium, and 91 per cent in Brazil, while official turnout in the elections for which respondents were surveyed was respectively 92 per cent, 88 per cent, and 80 per cent. Unsurprisingly, turnout is overestimated in our surveys, partly because abstainers are less willing to respond to political surveys while others are reluctant to admit that they did not vote (Selb and Munzert 2013). However, the patterns that are uncovered in studies of reported turnout are similar to those observed with validated turnout (Achen and Blais 2016).

Our central independent variable is the perceived sanction for abstention, or more precisely the perceived probability to incur a sanction if one does not vote. As explained in Section 3, we have three indicators of the perceived consequences of abstention: the perceived probability of having to fill out a form, pay a fine, and go to court if one does not vote. We first include these three indicators separately (models 1, 2, and 3), then include the three of them together (model 4), and finally use a combined measure, which is simply the mean of the three indicators (model 5). Our multivariate estimation includes age, sex, education, and political interest as controls.

The results of the logit regressions (presented in online Appendix F) show that, without exception, the coefficients of perceived sanction enforcement have the expected positive sign. In Brazil, however, the coefficients are smaller, and are not significantly different from zero for perceptions of having to fill out a form and going to court. Overall, thinking that one will have to pay a fine or not is what matters most.

To interpret the findings in more detail, we focus on the models with the summary indicator of perceived sanctions (i.e., the mean of citizens' perceptions that abstainers must fill out a form, pay a fine and have to go to court). In Figure 16, we show that the predicted probability of voting increases with the perceived probability of incurring a sanction in each of the three countries. In Australia, the impact of perceived sanctions is huge. Predicted turnout goes from 50 per cent when the probability of sanctions is deemed to be nil to 100 per cent when sanctions are judged to be certain. These results suggest that turnout would be 40 points lower in Australia if people thought that there would be no consequence at all to abstention (i.e., it would be 50 per cent instead of 90 per cent).

The findings are more muted in Belgium and Brazil. In Belgium, the propensity to vote goes from 87 per cent to 98 per cent as perceived sanctions move from nil to complete. According to these results, turnout among our sample of respondents would be 87 per cent instead of 93 per cent if everyone were convinced that there would be no sanction. As we saw in Section 3, many Belgians are not aware that the probability of a sanction is extremely small, and this misperception contributes to the high turnout observed in that country. But our data indicate that misperceptions are not the most crucial factor, as turnout would still be exceptionally high. This finding suggests that the presence of

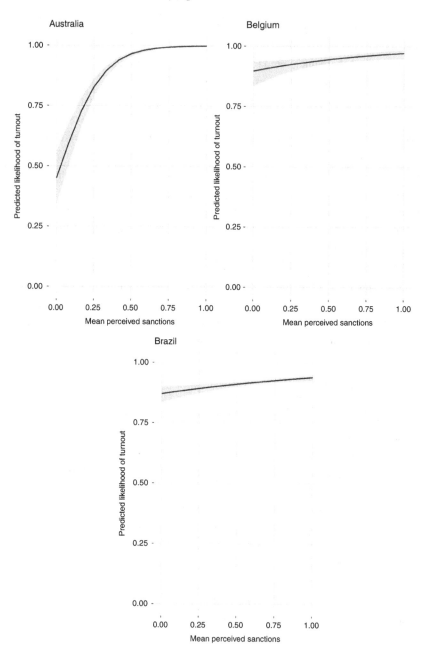

Figure 16 Predicted likelihood to vote, by perceived sanctions for abstention

Note: Estimates of three country-specific logistic regression models explaining intention to abstain if voting is voluntary. The estimates are based on model 5 in Tables 1, 2 and 3 in online Appendix F. The shaded area shows 95 per cent confidence intervals.

a compulsory voting law has led many Belgians to view voting as a moral obligation.

The situation in Brazil resembles that in Belgium. Our data suggest that the likelihood of voting increases from 85 per cent when someone thinks that there are certainly no sanctions when one abstains from voting to 93 per cent when the person believes that there are definitively sanctions (i.e., when respondents think they will certainly have to fill out a form, pay a fine, and go to court). These numbers are very similar to those observed in Belgium. In both countries, people are more likely to vote if they expect sanctions for abstention, especially fines, but the impact of sanctions and their enforcement is limited. What seems to matter the most is the public symbolic statement that voting is compulsory in the country. People are willing to obey the law, even a law with no teeth, and, in the case of Brazil, a law that they oppose.

5.5 Summary and Implications

Compulsory voting works remarkably well in our three countries. This is the main reason turnout is around 90 per cent in Australia and Belgium. Turnout is slightly lower in Brazil, but, given the socio-demographic profile of that country, we would expect a lower 'normal' turnout under voluntary voting. Therefore, we conclude that compulsory voting works in that country as well. Compulsory voting is also successful in reducing unequal participation, especially the education gap, though it only lessens the age gap in Australia. The largest effect of all is observed among those with little interest in politics, who would stay home under voluntary voting.

The big question concerns how this effect is produced, and the relative impact of enforced sanctions versus symbols. The first point to be made is that we need to examine not only objective facts, what sanctions are stipulated in the law or even numbers of fines, but also citizens' subjective perceptions about the probability of having to pay fines if one does not vote. As we have seen in Section 3, these perceptions are sometimes far from accurate.

We have confirmed the findings of prior research that sanctions and their enforcement matter. Everything else being equal, believing that one will have to pay a fine increases the probability of voting. But sanctions are far from fully explaining the impact of compulsory voting. In Belgium and Brazil, our data suggest that turnout would decline by only 5 or 6 percentage points if people were convinced that there would be no consequence to staying home.

We infer that symbols matter as much as sanctions. The mere presence of a law that tells people they are obliged to vote sends a powerful message that suffices to drive some to the polls, even if they know that they will not have to pay any fine. Belgium illustrates this, as turnout has declined only slightly since sanctions have been abandoned. This is partly because some Belgians still think that sanctions are enforced. Nevertheless, an overwhelming majority of those who know that they will definitely not have to pay a fine turn out.

Things are different in Australia. Our data suggest that about half the citizens would be inclined to abstain in the absence of sanctions, which suggests that sanctions matter more in that country. Yet, let us keep in mind that only 10 per cent of our respondents indicate that they would not vote if voting was voluntary. We infer that in that country as well the presence of compulsory voting has strengthened citizens' acceptance of the norm that voting is a civic duty. In each of the three countries, we conclude, compulsory voting works through a successful combination of symbols and sanctions.

6 The Consequences of Compulsory Voting

Compulsory voting increases election turnout – often dramatically. What other consequences does compulsory voting have for the political system? The 'secondary effects' of compulsory voting rules have already been highlighted in the literature. Considerable attention has been given to the impact of compulsory voting on the individuals' voting behaviour, with a focus on the determinants of vote choice (Singh 2010, 2021), random voting (Freire and Turgeon 2020), and casting ideologically consistent votes (Dassonneville et al. 2019; Selb and Lachat 2009). Other studies have examined the connection between compulsory voting and outcome variables that help citizens function in democracy, such as their political knowledge (Sheppard 2015; Shineman 2021), political attitudes like civic duty (Feitosa et al. 2020), satisfaction with democracy (Singh 2018) and support for authority (Singh 2021). A final set of studies focuses on whether countries that mandate turnout realize a better representation of the preferences and interests of the population, through a focus on who gets elected and the policies that governments enact (Bechtel et al. 2016; Carey and Horiuchi 2017; Fowler 2013).

The insights from these studies are important, as they go to the heart of what compulsory voting is designed to achieve: greater equity in how political elites respond to the demands of voters (Birch 2009; Brennan and Hill 2014; Engelen 2007). In this debate, opponents of compulsory voting argue that it undermines personal liberty and brings more uninformed voters to the polls. Such voters are more likely to cast random (Freire and Turgeon 2020) or inconsistent votes (Dassonneville et al. 2019; Selb and Lachat 2009), implying that citizens' preferences are not better represented under high mandatory turnout (Lever 2010; Volacu 2020). Others are more optimistic and argue that some of these effects are counterbalanced by the fact that compulsory voting incites voters to seek more information and gain more knowledge about party offerings (Shineman 2021).

This section evaluates claims about the political consequences of compulsory voting by shedding light on the impact that mobilizing these voters has on election outcomes. We start by reviewing previous work that has studied whether mobilizing under-represented groups results in differences in who gets elected. We pay attention to the possibility that compulsory voting alters the partisan composition of the legislature. We then empirically examine the ideological differences between voters who would and would not turn out to vote if voting was voluntary. Finally, we focus more directly on the vote choices of different groups of voters and evaluate which parties would win and lose if the three countries abolished compulsory voting.

6.1 Compulsory Voting and Political Equity

Advocates of compulsory voting generally do not consider boosting turnout as the ultimate goal but see it as a means to improve equity in whose interests are represented in politics. In a 1997 article, Lijphart advanced the argument that countries with voluntary voting attracted disproportionately larger numbers of better educated, more economically prosperous voters. In turn, parties in such settings pay more attention to those who consistently turn out to vote. By mandating turnout, the pool of voters who turnout becomes more diverse, which should encourage the parties to pay more attention to the interests of voters with lower socio-economic status.

There is some evidence to support this contention. Belgian research that simulated the effects of compulsory voting conducted immediately after Lijphart's original article supported his main findings (Hooghe and Pelleriaux 1998). In a later article, Lijphart (2001) elaborated on the policy consequences of compulsory voting by arguing that low turnout and the unequal representation of social groups made it easier for governments to support programs that favoured the better off and to ignore those that served the poor. Along the same lines, Hill (2006) – who relies on theoretical arguments and practical Australian experience – sees compulsory voting not only as a solution for low turnout but also as a device that creates more equitable policy outcomes.

A variety of studies have tested Lijphart's claims empirically. Several studies offer indications that compulsory voting results in more equitable public policies. In an examination of 43 countries, nine with compulsory voting, Jensen and Spoon (2011) conclude that compulsory-voting countries have more parliamentary parties and, most importantly, a larger ideological range of governments compared to voluntary-voting countries. They conclude that 'there is something qualitatively different about compulsory voting rules as compared to only increasing turnout' (p.707), suggesting that high turnout and compulsory voting are not necessarily similar in the effects they have on public policy. Similar conclusions are reached by Chong and Olivera (2008) and Fowler (2013). Finally, using Venezuela as a case study, Carey and Horiuchi (2017) show that the 1993 abolition of compulsory voting resulted in more unequal income distribution.

Other work offers less support for Lijphart's conclusions. Work on the Chilean case – a country that switched from compulsory to voluntary voting – shows that unless compulsory voting results in near-universal turnout there is no guarantee that the increase in turnout will be associated with smaller biases in who turns out to vote and who does not (Brieba and Bunker 2019). Furthermore, Kouba (2021), who studied the effects of the adoption of compulsory voting in Austro-Hungary at the beginning of the twentieth century, failed to find evidence that the introduction of mandatory voting reduced the class bias in electoral participation.

Other research on the effects of compulsory voting also fails to find support for equalization. Hoffman, León and Lombardi (2017) examine the staggered abolition of compulsory voting across the Austrian states to estimate its causal effects. They find that even though compulsory voting is associated with higher turnout, neither election outcomes nor patterns of government spending are affected by the change. Finally, by studying mass-elite congruence in a large set of democracies, Lupu and Warner (2021) find strong evidence that the rich are better represented than the poor across democracies but fail to find evidence that compulsory voting substantially reduces income differences in representation.

Supporters of compulsory voting argue that its impact on turnout is normatively desirable because – by increasing turnout – it reduces inequalities in representation and in the distribution of public goods. However, the empirical evidence to support this proposition is mixed. There are three explanations for the lack of a clear impact of compulsory voting on political equity. First, the effect of compulsory voting on turnout can be too limited to have downstream effects. Second, compulsory voting can fail to have equalizing effects if it increases turnout but does not substantially reduce inequalities in turnout. Third, the impact of compulsory voting on political equality assumes that mobilizing under-represented groups alters the outcome of elections and in this way who governs.

Our analyses of the effects of compulsory voting in Australia, Belgium, and Brazil in Section 5 have shown that even though it does not result in universal turnout, it is effective in increasing turnout and is associated with smaller biases in participation. What remains to be seen is whether these effects alter the outcome of elections. In what follows, we first review previous work that has specifically studied the connection between compulsory voting, turnout, and election outcomes. This overview lays the groundwork for an examination of the partisan effects of compulsory voting in Australia, Belgium and Brazil.

6.2 The Partisan Effects of Compulsory Voting

Does compulsory voting deliver a partisan advantage to any of the political parties? A large literature has studied the connection between voter turnout and election outcomes. The assumption in much of this work is that high election turnout benefits parties of the left, while lower turnout benefits parties of the right. It is argued that this occurs because higher turnout brings to the polls voters from lower socio-economic backgrounds, who are the natural electoral base of centre-left parties. Conversely, lower turnout tends to overrepresent more prosperous voters, who form the natural electoral base for centre-right parties (Pacek and Radcliff 1995). Given that lower socio-economic voters are less likely to vote in low-turnout elections, this should reduce support for parties that defend the interests of working-class voters (DeNardo 1980).

Evidence to support this proposition has come from countries as diverse as Germany (Arnold and Freier 2016), Korea (Kang 2019), the Netherlands (Eisinga, Grotenhuis and Pelzer 2012) and the US (Gomez, Hansford and Krause 2007). However, in most cases the size of the effect is small. While these studies confirm that high turnout benefits centre-left parties, the literature is in fact divided. Several scholars conclude that the connection between turnout and election outcomes is weak. Focusing on the Canadian case, Rubenson et al. (2007) use election survey data to simulate the outcome of the 2000 Canadian federal election under full participation. They find that shifts in vote share between the actual and simulated election results are consistently small. Godbout and Turgeon (2019), adopting a different strategy, find some differences between voters and non-voters. They show that non-voters hold preferences that are more conservative than voters. Other studies have used the consistent decline in election turnout in advanced democracies from the 1980s onward to measure the electoral effects of differential turnout. Their conclusion is that the biases in party support due to differential turnout are exaggerated. In an exhaustive comparative study of differential turnout, Lutz and Marsh (2007; see also Nagel and McNulty 1996) come to the same conclusion.

Previous research has therefore found mixed evidence for the theory that the left benefits from high turnout. The lack of a consensus likely stems from contextual factors that condition the ways in which voters choose parties. As a result, 'turnout effects vary both across countries and between successive elections' (Remer-Bollow, Bernhagen and Rose 2019: 91). Furthermore, some work suggests that a distinction between traditional left and new left parties blurs important variations in who benefits and who loses in high turnout elections. Bol and Giani (2021: 450), who rely on imputation to simulate the outcomes of European elections under full participation, conclude that an increase in turnout 'does not change the overall score of left-wing parties, but would affect its composition, favouring social democratic parties at the expenses of extreme left and green parties'.

Such findings about the partisan effects of high turnout, however, do not provide strong empirical evidence to infer the partisan effects of compulsory voting. As argued by Singh (2021: 53) 'an electorate that approached full turnout voluntarily would differ meaningfully from one that did so due [to] the threat of legal sanctions for abstentions.' Fortunately, several studies examine the partisan advantages or disadvantages that may accrue to a compulsory voting system. Australia has attracted particular attention in this regard. An early study by Mackerras and McAllister (1999) simulated national turnout based on a survey question asking intention to vote under a voluntary system. They concluded that there was a consistent benefit to the centre-left Labor party of around 5 percentage points due to compulsory voting.

Using surveys to measure voting intention under different voting rules has been criticized by Jackman (1999: 43), who argues that survey samples are already skewed towards voters who are more likely to turn out and to voters who are more susceptible to social desirability bias. However, even after taking these factors into account, Jackman still finds a 3 percentage point advantage to the centre-right Liberal party if compulsory voting were to be abolished. Relying on a different approach and leveraging as-if-random variation in the introduction of compulsory voting across the Australian states, Fowler (2013) provides causal estimates of its partisan effect. In line with survey-based research on the Australian case, he concludes that 'increased voter turnout can dramatically alter election outcomes' and estimates the advantage to Labor due to compulsory voting to be around 7 percentage points (Fowler 2013: 160).

In contrast to studies analysing the partisan effects of compulsory voting in Australia, research on the Belgian case has found little indication that abolishing mandatory voting would result in meaningful shifts in election outcomes. Hooghe and Pelleriaux (1998: 423), who use information on Belgian voters' intended participation under voluntary voting, find that 'parties relying on a high-status electorate (ecologists, conservatives) gained votes, while parties relying on an electorate with little formal education (socialists, extreme right) would lose votes.' However, they also observe that shifts are generally very small, with parties winning or losing 1 to 2 per cent of the vote at most. Based on these results, they conclude that 'abolishing compulsory voting would not fundamentally affect the power structure within the Belgian polity.' Selb and Lachat (2009: 590), who also use election survey data from Belgium, conclude that there are 'barely any differences' between election outcomes under compulsory voting and a counterfactual scenario without mandatory voting.

Other work has cast light on the partisan effects of compulsory voting by studying real-life examples of countries that abolished compulsory voting. The abolition of compulsory voting in the Netherlands in 1970 provides a natural experiment to compare voting in a pre and post-compulsory voting electoral system within an advanced democracy. Turnout was consistently above 90 per cent before the change, and only 68 per cent in the provincial election organized shortly after the switch to voluntary voting. In the parliamentary elections that were organized shortly after the change to voluntary voting, turnout was higher (it was 79 per cent in 1971 and 83 per cent in 1972), but still more than 10 percentage points lower than the rates observed under compulsory voting (Irwin 1974). In examining the partisan effects of the abolition of compulsory voting, Miller and Dassonneville (2016: 132) find that the change 'led to an increase in the vote share of Dutch social democratic parties and a decrease in the vote share won by minor and extreme parties.' The shifts that they observe, however, are small.

In summary, while there is a clear theoretical expectation that centre-left parties should do better under compulsory voting, the empirical evidence is mixed and generally points to small effects at best. Three reasons can be given to explain this apparent lack of strong partisan effects.

First, it might be that even though higher turnout results in reduced sociodemographic inequalities in participation, the political and partisan preferences of voters and abstainers are similar.

Second, even if voters' and abstainers' issue positions differ, those positions are not necessarily central to their vote choice. The lack of a strong connection between issue positions and vote choices could also explain why research on referendums – where issues are central and party cues are weaker – suggests that differential turnout can be important. For example, in the 2016 UK Brexit referendum, leave-leaning voters were more likely to turnout compared to remain-leaning voters (Rudolph 2020). In the 2018 Australian same-sex marriage plebiscite (conducted under a voluntary voting system), supporters of reform were also more likely to turnout to vote than opponents (McAllister and Snagovsky 2018). Work on the Swiss case also shows strong evidence of a connection between compulsory voting and support for left-wing policies in referenda. Bechtel et al. (2016) find that sanctioned mandatory voting increases support for left-wing policies by up to 20 percentage points.

Third, as argued by Ferwerda (2014), electoral systems create conditions that mute the partisan effects of changes in turnout and hence of the introduction or abolition of compulsory voting. In settings of multi-party competition, significant partisan swings require both a large change in turnout and a substantial skew in the partisan preferences of voters and non-voters. The more competition there is, the more dispersed are the votes of those who would abstain under voluntary voting. As a result, no single party would lose or win much when moving from mandatory to voluntary voting.

6.3 Ideological Differences between Reluctant and Willing Voters

Before examining the impact of compulsory voting in terms of election outcomes, we take a close look at the ideological preferences of those who would vote even if it was voluntary and those who would not. We label the former group as 'willing voters' and in line with Dassonneville et al. (2019) we refer to the latter as 'reluctant voters'. The belief that compulsory voting rules improves the representation of under-represented groups assumes that mandatory voting mobilizes groups that would otherwise not turn out to vote, and that the interests of these groups differ from those of citizens who would vote even under voluntary voting.

Our analyses have already shown that the socio-demographic profile of reluctant voters (i.e., those who would abstain under voluntary voting) differs from that of those who would turn out to vote if compulsory voting was abolished. As Section 5 demonstrated, the less educated and females especially have a higher tendency to abstain. The consequences of these differential turnout rates for the political representation of these groups, however, depend on whether their values and interests differ in meaningful ways from those of willing voters. Do reluctant voters have policy preferences that differ from those of willing voters?

Our expectation is that reluctant voters take more left-wing positions than willing voters. We start our analyses with a focus on respondents' self-placement on a left-right scale, which is the only measure of ideology that was included in all three surveys. To distinguish between 'reluctant voters' and 'willing voters', we make use of the survey item asking respondents to indicate their likelihood of turning out to vote if it was voluntary. The response categories were 'definitely not', 'probably not', 'might/might not', 'probably' and 'definitely'. For the purposes of our analyses, we focus on the contrast between those who would definitely or probably not vote (i.e., 'reluctant voters') and those indicating that they would probably or definitely vote (i.e., 'willing voters'). We omit respondents who chose the middle option from the analyses.

Table 5 Mean left-right placement of reluctant and willing voters in Australia, Belgium, and Brazil

Country	Reluctant voters	Willing voters	Difference
Australia	5.08	5.40	0.32
Belgium	5.43	5.26	−0.17
Brazil	5.47	5.81	0.34***

Note: Mean left-right position on a zero (left) to 10 (right) of reluctant and willing voters respectively. Results from a t-test are reported in the 'Difference' column. Significance level: ***$p < 0.01$.

The results in Table 5 show no difference in the ideological positions of reluctant and willing voters in Australia or Belgium. The positions of both sets of voters are always close to the ideological centre of the left-right scale. In Australia, those who would probably or definitely turn out to vote under voluntary voting are somewhat more right-leaning than those intending to abstain, but the difference is not statistically different from zero. In Belgium, the direction of the difference is even opposite to our expectations, but also not significantly different from zero. By contrast, there is a significant difference between the two groups in Brazil. The difference is in the expected direction, with willing voters placing themselves significantly more to the political right than their reluctant counterparts. In Brazil as well, however, the size of the difference between the two groups is limited. Moreover, Oliveira and Turgeon (2015) show that most Brazilians do not understand the meanings of left and right so that the small difference uncovered in Table 5 may not mean much.

Party competition is increasingly characterized as multi-dimensional (Hooghe and Marks 2018; Kriesi et al. 2006). As a result, a focus on citizens' positions on a single left-right dimension can mask important variations in the preferences of reluctant and willing voters on specific ideological dimensions. Unfortunately, the survey data do not allow us to systematically study citizens' positions concerning moral issues or the environment. However, given that the Australian and Belgian surveys both included the questions from the fifth module of the Comparative Study of Electoral Systems, these two datasets include comparable information on citizens' attitudes towards immigration and their views on the government's role in reducing income inequalities.

In Tables 6 and 7 we examine respondents' positions on immigration and economic intervention, two issues that do not necessarily map closely onto respondents' left-right positions (de Vries et al. 2013). Details on the question wording of these items can be found in online Appendix G, but it is important to

Table 6 Issue positions of reluctant and willing voters in Australia

Issue	Reluctant voters	Willing voters	Difference
Immigration harms the economy	0.46	0.31	−0.15***
Immigration threatens our culture	0.46	0.35	−0.11**
Immigration increases crime	0.50	0.44	−0.07
Gov. should not take measures to reduce income inequalities	0.28	0.39	0.11***

Note: Mean issue positions (on scales that range between 0 and 1) of reluctant and willing voters respectively. Results from a t-test are reported in the 'Difference' column. Significance level: **p < 0.01, ***p < 0.001.

Table 7 Issue positions of reluctant and willing voters in Belgium

Issue	Reluctant voters	Willing voters	Difference
Immigration harms the economy	0.65	0.53	−0.12***
Immigration threatens our culture	0.72	0.55	−0.17***
Immigration increases crime	0.70	0.55	−0.15***
Gov. should not take measures to reduce income inequalities	0.16	0.27	0.11***

Note: Mean issue positions (on scales that range between 0 and 1) of reluctant and willing voters respectively. Results from a t-test are reported in the 'Difference' column. Significance level: ***p < 0.001.

indicate that we scaled all items to run from 0 to 1, with higher values corresponding to more right-wing attitudes.

In Table 6 we list the results from the Australian survey, while Table 7 does the same for Belgium. In both countries we find some evidence that the views of reluctant voters (those who would not turnout under voluntary voting) differ from those who would vote even if it were not mandatory. The sign of the differences is also consistent in the two countries, indicating that reluctant voters are significantly more right-wing in terms of immigration and more left-wing in terms of the economy.

Our analyses suggest that when focusing on a general left-right dimension, there are few indications that the ideological positions of reluctant voters differ meaningfully from those of willing voters. Only in Brazil do we find that those who would turn out under voluntary voting take positions that are significantly more right-wing than those who would not turn out to vote if it were not mandatory. Based on such patterns, it might be concluded that abolishing compulsory voting, and the decline in participation that would result, would not weaken the extent to which abstainers' interests are represented in politics. A focus on a single left-right dimension, however, masks important differences in the views that citizens hold on different policy dimensions. Even though the data are limited, we show that when we examine attitudes on specific issues like immigration or the role of government in reducing inequalities, there is some evidence that those who would abstain under voluntary voting have views that differ from those of willing voters.

6.4 Partisan Differences between Reluctant and Willing Voters

To study the counterfactual of what election outcomes would look like if voting were voluntary in Australia, Belgium, and Brazil, we again rely on respondents' self-reported intention to turnout under voluntary voting. We assume that respondents who indicate that they would 'probably' or 'definitely' not vote would abstain from voting. We then calculate the support that different parties receive among the remaining respondents and compare that with their shares of reported votes in the total sample, that is, under compulsory voting. As an alternative approach, we also conduct a simulation based on weighting, which results in differences that are generally more muted (see online Appendix H).

We start the analyses with a focus on the partisan effects of compulsory voting in Australia. The top panel in Figure 17 shows the reported vote choices of respondents for the 2019 federal election, while the bottom panel shows the distribution of reported votes while excluding reluctant voters. Comparing the two distributions suggests that the partisan effects of abolishing compulsory voting in Australia would be minimal. There are fewer voters who would opt for 'other' parties, but the size of the swings for parties is at most 1 percentage point. Neither the right-wing Liberal and National parties nor the left-wing Labor and Green parties seem affected by reluctant voters not turning out to vote. In contrast to earlier work on the Australian case (Fowler 2013; Jackman 1999; Mackerras and McAllister 1999), the data for the 2019 election offer few indications of a partisan effect of compulsory voting.

We next examine the partisan effects of compulsory voting in Belgium. To take into account the different language-based party systems in Belgium (Brack and Pilet 2010), we assess shifts in vote shares in the Flemish and Walloon subsamples separately. The Belgian survey included an option to indicate whether respondents intended to cast a blank or invalid vote. Quite logically, the share of voters indicating such an intention is substantially lower when we

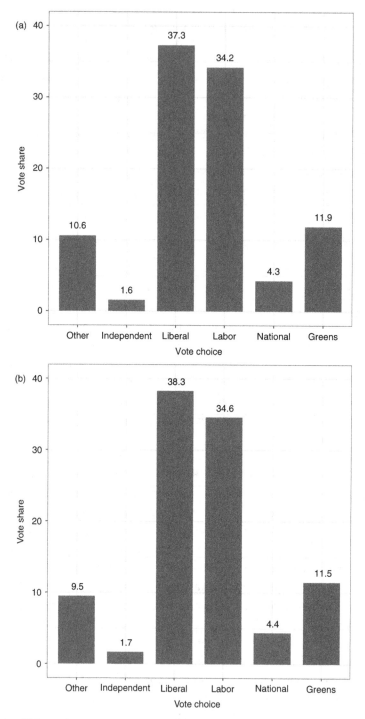

Figure 17 Bars show the per cent of the vote that different parties obtain among all voters (top panel) and when excluding reluctant voters (bottom panel) – Australia

Note: Bars show the per cent of voters choosing a particular vote option among those reporting a vote.

exclude reluctant voters.[12] For our analyses of the partisan effects of compulsory voting, we code those respondents as missing, because their votes are not affecting the partisan composition of the legislature.

Figure 18 shows the data for the Flemish respondents, with the distribution of vote shares among all voters in the 2019 federal elections in panel a and the distributions when excluding reluctant voters in panel b. In Flanders, the data suggest that shifts would be small. There are only three categories for which the difference between panel a and panel b is larger than one percentage point. The analysis suggests that abolishing compulsory voting would imply a decline in the vote share of the extreme-right Vlaams Belang (VB), with Figure 18 showing a drop of 2 percentage points between the full sample and the sample excluding reluctant voters. On the other hand, Figure 18 shows increases in vote shares for the Christian-Democrats (+2 percentage points) and the Green party (Groen) (+2 percentage points). Overall, Figure 18 does not offer clear indications of left-right dynamics in the partisan effects of compulsory voting. The extreme-right would lose a bit, but there is also an increase in the vote of the centre-right Christian-Democrats (CD&V). For other right-wing parties, like the N-VA, the data from the 2019 survey suggest that compulsory voting does not affect its electoral strength. At the other end of the ideological spectrum, the data hint at some advantage for small left-wing parties (PVDA and Groen) but no effect for the Social-Democrats (SP.a).

In the Walloon subsample too, the data suggest that blank and invalid voting would all but disappear under voluntary voting.[13] In terms of shifts in party vote shares, Figure 19, provides some indications of partisan effects of compulsory voting. There are three parties for which the difference in vote shares between panel a (full sample) and panel b (excluding reluctant voters) amounts to more than 2 percentage points. Figure 19 suggests that moving to voluntary voting would increase the vote share of the centre-right Liberal Party MR (+2 percentage points) and the Green party Ecolo (+2 percentage points). On the other hand, the social-democratic party PS appears to lose votes when it is assumed that reluctant voters would not turn out to vote (−2 percentage points). These shifts are in line with the work of Bol and Giani (2021), who argue that compulsory voting benefits social democratic parties but harms green parties. The results again underline the fact that the partisan effects of compulsory voting cannot be reduced to simple left-right dynamics.

---

[12] In the Flemish subsample, the share of blank/invalid votes drops from 2.0 per cent of all vote intentions in the full sample to 0.2 per cent when excluding reluctant voters.

[13] Specifically, 6.0 per cent of all respondents indicated they voted blank or invalid, while only 0.1 per cent do so when reluctant voters are coded as missing.

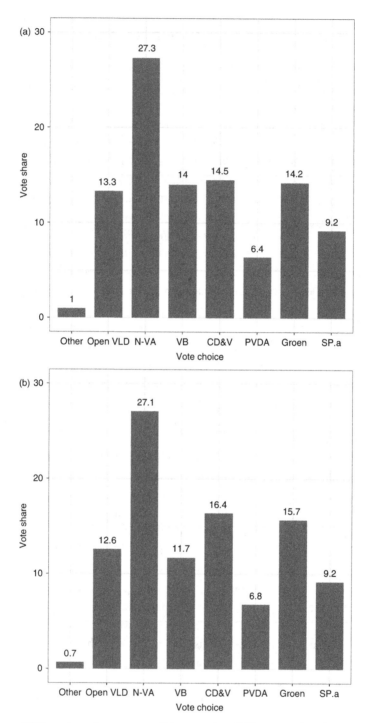

Figure 18 Bars show the per cent of the vote that different parties obtain among all voters (top panel) and when excluding reluctant voters (bottom panel) – Belgium (Flanders)

Note: Bars show the per cent of voters choosing a particular vote option among those reporting a non-blank/invalid vote.

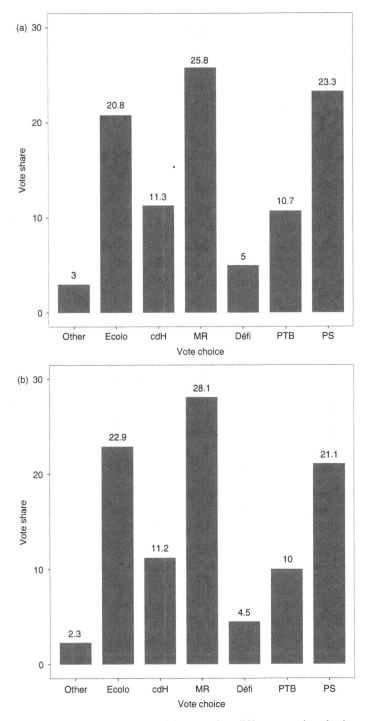

Figure 19 Bars show the per cent of the vote that different parties obtain among all voters (top panel) and when excluding reluctant voters (bottom panel) – Belgium (Wallonia)

Note: Bars show the per cent of voters choosing a particular vote option among those reporting a non-blank/invalid vote.

Finally, we turn to the case of Brazil. As was the case for the Belgian data, respondents in the survey were offered a blank/invalid option in the vote choice question. Unsurprisingly, the proportion of respondents who indicated they cast a blank/invalid vote is substantially lower when we exclude reluctant voters.[14] We coded these voters as missing to gauge the partisan impact of compulsory voting. Figure 20 shows the distribution of respondents' party votes. Given that the Brazilian survey was fielded during the 2018 presidential election, our focus is on first-round support for the presidential candidates. We again compare vote choice for the full sample with just those who said they would vote if it was voluntary. In contrast to what we observed in Australia and Belgium, the data for Brazil indicate that one party would have done much better if the 2018 elections had been held under voluntary voting: Jair Bolsonaro's PSL party. More specifically, while 44 per cent of all respondents in the sample indicate they voted for Bolsonaro's party in the first round of the presidential election, if we exclude reluctant voters the party's share of support increases to 51 per cent (+7 percentage points). For the other parties, differences are minimal, though it is noteworthy that the smaller parties (which we grouped in the 'other' category) would get fewer votes if reluctant voters did not vote. In Brazil, therefore, a radical-right option would benefit most from a change to voluntary voting, which contrasts with our findings for the Vlaams Belang in Flanders.

6.5 Summary and Implications

The impact of compulsory voting in increasing turnout is well established. By mandating voting, more citizens turnout to vote and turnout becomes more equal, most notably in terms of education. But whether this equalization of participation also spurs more equality in representation depends on the political and partisan preferences of those who would abstain if voting was not mandated.

By systematically analysing the political preferences and the vote choices of citizens who would not vote under voluntary voting ('reluctant voters') and comparing them with those of citizens who would turn out to vote ('willing voters'), we shed light on the equalizing effects of compulsory voting in our three countries. Our results indicate that to assess the partisan effects of compulsory voting it is important to move beyond a focus on a single left-right dimension. Depending on the types of issues that one assesses, reluctant voters either do or do not hold political views that differ meaningfully from

---

[14] In the full sample, 9.4 per cent indicated they casted a blank/invalid vote, when excluding reluctant voters there are only 2.5 per cent blank/invalid voters left.

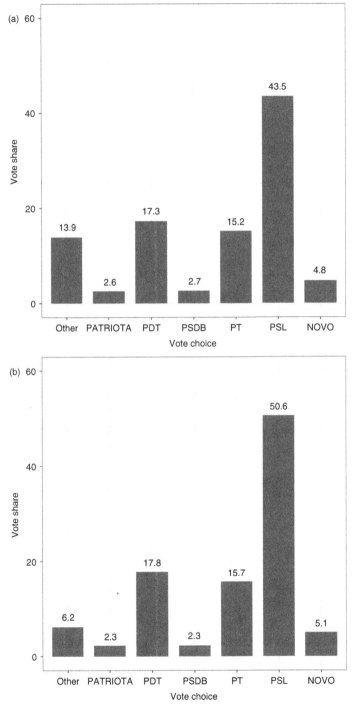

Figure 20 Bars show the per cent of the vote that different parties obtain among all voters (top panel) and when excluding reluctant voters (bottom panel) – Brazil

Note: Bars show the per cent of voters choosing a particular vote option among those reporting a non-blank/invalid vote.

those of willing voters. The implication is that when the issues on which reluctant voters hold different views are politically salient and structure voters' electoral choices, the mobilization of reluctant voters can substantially change election outcomes.

Because the issues and dimensions that shape citizens' vote choices have been found to change over time and differ between countries (van der Brug and Rekker 2021), predicting the direction of the partisan effects of compulsory voting is challenging. This is clear from our analyses, which show effects that are unique to each of the three cases that we investigate. We find no evidence of partisan effects in Australia, modest shifts across the ideological spectrum in Flanders and Wallonia, and a strong impact on support for a radical-right party in Brazil.

7 Conclusion

Citizens in Australia, Belgium, and Brazil are obliged, by law, to turn out to vote. While the three countries share a compulsory voting system, what form this obligation takes, how it is sanctioned, and whether and how it is enforced differ between each. In practice, the implementation of compulsory voting is more nuanced and less strict than is stipulated by law.

In Australia, where non-voters risk a fine there are relatively few voters who effectively pay a fine. The following quote, taken from an interview that the *New York Times* conducted in the framework of their research on compulsory voting in Australia, illustrates this point:

> I once accidentally missed a local election. I was sent a letter asking me why I didn't vote. I wrote back, explaining I was commuting out of town for work and missed the local ads, and they didn't fine me.
>
> —Voter from Perth, as quoted in the *New York Times* on 22 October 2018 (Rychter 2018)

In Belgium public officials have informed the public that prosecuting offenders was not a priority for the courts and that abstainers would not have to pay a fine, leading an influential journalist to refer to the Belgian system as 'optional compulsory voting' (Gerlache 2012). In Brazil, even though the enforcement of compulsory voting is strict, it is only when a non-voter needs a service from the state that they are asked to pay a small fine.

We have provided a rich description of compulsory voting rules in Australia, Belgium, and Brazil, and surveyed citizens in these three countries about their views of compulsory voting. The survey data allowed us to study comparatively the perceptions that citizens hold about compulsory voting and how these perceptions influence their behaviour. We were able to examine what citizens think are the consequences of abstention, analyse how much support there is for compulsory voting and where that support is strongest/weakest. The survey data also allowed us to shed light on the mobilizing impact of compulsory voting, allowing us to scrutinize which individuals and parties are most affected by compulsory voting.

In what follows, we first review the main findings that were presented in the preceding sections. We then discuss some limitations of our work, and how future research could address those limitations and expand on our work. We end by discussing the broader implications of our findings.

7.1 Summary of Our Findings

The three countries differ markedly in terms of who compulsory voting applies to, the nature of the sanctions, and enforcement. In Australia, non-voters receive a notice asking them to either provide an explanation for their apparent failure to vote or pay a fine. Given that most reasonable excuses for non-voting are accepted, in practice very few Australians are fined. In Belgium, in contrast, excuses for non-voting must be sent to the judge before election day. But those who fail to do so do not face any consequences. This is a result of the fact that the judiciary has been asked not to reprimand abstainers. Finally, in Brazil enforcement is strict but does not take place immediately and there is no notification from the authorities. Furthermore, the fine is extremely small. The main takeaways from our country descriptions of compulsory voting are that compulsory voting has very different rules and practices, and that the consequences for abstaining are not severe.

Citizens, however, are very uncertain and often misinformed about the ways in which compulsory voting is enforced. We showed that many people overestimate the consequences of abstention. To some extent, this likely results from the disconnect between what the law stipulates and its implementation. But there is also much misinformation. For example, 13 per cent of Belgians think they will have to go to court if they do not turn out to vote. In Brazil, where voting is compulsory for voters within a specific age range, voters have a good sense of who is required to vote by law but most are uninformed about how exactly the criteria apply.

We found that there is strong support for compulsory voting in Australia (75 per cent of respondents are in favour or strongly in favour), moderate approval in Belgium (54 per cent) and weak agreement in Brazil (30 per cent). This finding is consistent with the view that compulsory voting is weakly institutionalized in Brazil, where electoral democracy is still not firmly established. The socio-demographic profiles of citizens who are in favour of compulsory voting also differ from one country to another. In this regard, the association with higher education is noteworthy. In Australia and Belgium, we found that being highly educated is associated with higher levels of support for compulsory voting. In Brazil, in contrast, where compulsory voting is a contested norm, being highly educated significantly reduces the extent to which a respondent is in favour of compulsory voting. We also explored the presence of partisan differences and found few indications that citizens' political preferences are meaningfully connected with support for the institution of compulsory voting.

We then shifted the focus to examining the impact of compulsory voting. We showed that compulsory voting is effective in mobilizing citizens to turnout. We also presented evidence that suggests compulsory voting increases turnout through a combination of sanctions and symbolic effects. Specifically, we find that in each of the three countries, the higher a citizen perceives the cost of abstention to be, the more likely they are to vote. However, even those who believe that abstention is not sanctioned are very likely to turn out to vote.

Finally, we asked respondents to indicate how likely they would be to vote under voluntary voting rules to shed light on the downstream effects of compulsory voting. We used respondents' answers to this survey item to categorize them as 'reluctant' or 'willing' voters. Our analyses found that these two groups of voters are very similar in terms of their left-right self-placement. However, on more specific economic issues or issues related to immigration, reluctant and willing voters in Australia and Belgium appear to take significantly different positions. When examining in more depth which parties seem to benefit from compulsory voting, the results do not point to a single narrative that applies to the three countries. Instead, we showed that abolishing compulsory voting would not benefit any of the parties in Australia, would result in limited shifts in Belgium, but would be more consequential in Brazil.

7.2 Limitations and Future Research

Our research brings important insights into the concrete workings of compulsory voting in countries that mandate voting. Our analyses of the survey data allowed us to identify which sections of the electorate are more in favour of compulsory voting in each of these countries, but also which citizens are most affected by it – and why. These are important contributions, but at the same time we understand our research is limited and that more research on the topic is needed.

To gain insights into how compulsory voting works in practice, how citizens perceive it, and how it affects them, we chose to collect survey data. This approach entails two important limitations. First, citizens' survey responses suffer from measurement error and introduce bias. In part this is a consequence of the fact that the respondents we survey are not perfectly representative of the electorate, with non-voters especially being under-represented in our surveys. But there are also reasons to think that responses include error, and that participants are inclined to overreport turnout (Selb and Munzert 2013). While we admit that this is a limitation, in the absence of information that would allow validating respondents' turnout in the three countries, relying on self-reported turnout information is the only feasible way to examine the association between citizens' perceptions of compulsory voting and their political behaviour.

Second, with the observational data at hand we can provide a rich description of attitudes and the association between attitudes and reported behaviour – but we cannot infer causality. In recent years, scholarly interest in the topic of compulsory voting has grown substantially (for a literature review, see Singh 2021). Several of these studies use designs that are well suited to estimate causal effects. For example, they leverage the staggered introduction or abolition of compulsory voting to estimate its effect through difference-in-difference analysis (Bechtel et al. 2016; Fowler 2013; Hoffman et al. 2017). Alternatively, they use 'as-if-random' age-cutoffs in countries like Brazil to estimate how compulsory voting affects individual voters (Cepaluni and Hidalgo 2016; Turgeon and Blais 2021). Finally, researchers have relied on synthetic control methods to obtain a causal estimate of the impact of abolishing compulsory voting for citizens' attitudes (Feitosa et al. 2020) or party behaviour (Singh 2019, 2021). In contrast to this stream of studies, we cannot ascertain causality. We believe, however, that our descriptive survey-based research provides an important complement to studies that examine the causal effects of compulsory voting

Another limitation relates to the design of our survey questions. We sought to collect data that would be comparable across the three countries studied. This implied a reliance on questions that could be asked in each of the three countries and that therefore had to be sufficiently broad. That is why our questions asked about three potential consequences of non-voting: paying a fine, filling a form, and going to court. Future research should go in more depth and include questions that are tailored to each of the countries. In Australia, for example, it would be useful to ask whether citizens know which excuses for non-voting are acceptable. In Belgium, it would be worth adding questions to disentangle whether citizens conflate the consequences of non-voting after the election from the options they have preceding the election if they anticipate not being able to cast a vote. Furthermore, it would be most interesting to gather data on citizens' knowledge of sanctions for assigned counters and assessors not showing up on election day. Given that these sanctions *are* enforced, citizens might assume from this information that sanctions for non-voting too are enforced. Finally, in Brazil more specific survey questions would be useful to get a sense of whether people know which services are not available to abstainers (until a fine is duly paid).

7.3 How Does Compulsory Voting Work?

Our goal with this Element was to better understand citizens' views and perceptions of compulsory voting. In contrast to much previous work on the topic, that takes a broad comparative perspective and studies how compulsory-voting countries compare to voluntary-voting countries, we studied in-depth the dynamics of the institution *within* compulsory-voting countries. By doing so, we have gained important insights about the practice of compulsory voting, and citizens' perceptions of it.

Our research finds that there is no single system of compulsory voting, and that states have many tools to mandate voting and can be flexible in how they respond to non-compliance. We have also shown that in each of the three countries, all considered to be fairly strict in terms of compulsory voting, the actual sanctions for non-voting are either small or not effectively applied. It is therefore astonishing to see that compulsory voting is so effective in increasing turnout in the three countries. Our analyses show that high compliance is in part a function of citizens' overestimating the likelihood that they will face sanctions when they abstain. But sanctions are not the full story, which suggests that compulsory voting works through a combination of sanctions and symbolic effects. Future work should therefore pay at least as much attention to symbols as to sanctions.

While a focus on citizens' views allows bringing new insights to the study of compulsory voting, a citizen perspective is also limited. We know that the impacts of abolishing compulsory voting do not depend exclusively on how citizens would alter their behaviour under voluntary voting rules. Political parties too would likely adapt their strategies (Bugarin and Portugal 2015; Singh 2021). Singh (2019), for example, shows that a change from mandatory to voluntary voting rules leads parties to rely more on programmatic vote-seeking strategies and that it reduces the extent to which parties engage in clientelism. The implication is that the changes in citizen behaviour that would result from a change in the rules does not only depend on how citizens anticipate they would act, but also on changes in party behaviour and citizens' reactions to the behaviour of parties.

References

Achen, C. and Blais, A. (2016). 'Intention to vote, reported vote, and validated vote'. In Elking, J. A. and Farrell, D. M. (eds.), *The act of voting: Identities, institutions and locale*. London: Routledge, pp. 195–209.

Agência Câmara (2015). 'Câmara rejeita voto facultativo e mantém obrigatoriedade atual'. www.camara.leg.br/noticias/461372-camara-rejeita-voto-facultativo-e-mantem-obrigatoriedade-atual/ (last accessed on 30 November 2022).

Agência Senado (2017). 'Propostas tornam o voto facultativo no Brasil'. www12.senado.leg.br/noticias/audios/2017/05/propostas-tornam-o-voto-facultativo-no-brasil (last consulted on 30 November 2022).

Ajzen, I., Fisbein, M., Lohmann, S., and Albarracín, D. (2018). 'The influence of attitudes on behavior'. In Albarracín, D. and Johnson, B. T. (eds.), *The handbook of attitudes*, vol. 1, 2nd ed. New York: Routledge, pp. 197–255.

Arnold, F. and Freier, R. (2016). 'Only conservatives are voting in the rain: Evidence from German local and state elections'. *Electoral Studies*, 41, 216–21.

Barber, S. (2016). 'Federal election results 1901–2016'. https://apo.org.au/sites/default/files/resource-files/2017-03/apo-nid75062.pdf (last consulted on 25 January 2022).

Bechtel, M. M., Hangartner, D., and Schmid, L. (2016). 'Does compulsory voting increase support for leftist policy?' *American Journal of Political Science*, 60(3), 752–67.

Bennett, S. C. (2005). *Compulsory voting in Australian national elections*. Canberra: Parliament of Australia Research Debrief.

Berinsky, A. (2017). 'Rumors and health care reform: Experiments in political misinformation'. *British Journal of Political Science*, 47(2), 241–62.

Bethell, L. (2000). 'Politics in Brazil: From elections without democracy to democracy without citizenship'. *Daedalus*, 129(2), 1–27.

Birch, S. (2009). *Full participation: A comparative study of compulsory voting*. New York: United Nations University Press.

Blais, A. (2006). 'What affects voter turnout?' *Annual Review of Political Science*, 9, 111–25.

Blais, A. and Anduiza, E. (2013). 'Voter turnout'. In Vallelly, R. (ed.), *Oxford bibliographies in political science*. New York: Oxford University Press. www.oxfordbibliographies.com/display/document/obo-9780199756223/obo-9780199756223-0066.xml.

Blais, A. and Dobrzynska, A. (1998). 'Turnout in electoral democracies'. *European Journal of Political Research*, 33(2), 239–61.

Blais, A. and Daoust J.-F. (2020). *The motivation to vote: Explaining electoral participation.* Vancouver: UBC Press.

Bol, D. and Giani, M. (2021). 'It's a (coarsened exact) match! Non-parametric imputation of European abstainers' vote'. *Political Science Research and Methods*, 9(2), 445–50.

Bouhon, F. and Reuchamps, M. (eds.) (2018). *Les systems électoraux de la Belgique.* Brussels: Bruylant.

Brack, N. and Pilet, J.-B. (2010). 'One country, two party systems? The 2009 Belgian regional elections'. *Regional and Federal Studies*, 20(4–5), 549–59.

Brennan, J. and Hill, L. (2014). *Compulsory voting: For and against.* Cambridge: Cambridge University Press.

Brieba, D. and Bunker, K. (2019). 'Voter equalization and turnout bias after electoral reform: Evidence from Chile's voluntary voting law'. *Latin American Politics and Society*, 61(4), 23–46.

Broockman, D. E. and Butler, D. M. (2017). 'The causal effects of elite position-taking on voter attitudes: Field experiments with elite communication'. *American Journal of Political Science*, 61(1), 208–21.

Bugarin, M. and Portugal, A. (2015). 'Should voting be mandatory? The effect of compulsory voting rules on candidates' political platforms'. *Journal of Applied Economics*, 18(1), 1–19.

Carey, J. M. and Horiuchi, Y. (2017). 'Compulsory voting and income inequality: Evidence for Lijphart's proposition from Venezuela'. *Latin American Politics and Society*, 59, 122–44.

Cepaluni, G. and Hidalgo, F. D. (2016). 'Compulsory voting can increase political inequality: Evidence from Brazil'. *Political Analysis*, 24(2), 273–80.

Chapman, E. B. (2019). 'The distinctive value of elections and the case for compulsory voting'. *American Journal of Political Science*, 63(1), 101–12.

Chong, A. and Olivera, M. (2008). 'Does compulsory voting help equalize incomes?' *Economics & Politics*, 20(3), 391–415.

Converse, P. E. (1964). *The nature of belief systems in mass publics.* New York: Free Press.

Dassonneville, R., Feitosa, F., Hooghe, M., Lau, R. R., and Stiers, D. (2019). 'Compulsory voting rules, reluctant voters and ideological proximity voting'. *Political Behavior*, 41(1), 209–30.

Dassonneville, R. and Kostelka, F. (2021). 'The cultural sources of the gender gap in voter turnout'. *British Journal of Political Science*, 51(3), 1040–61.

Dassonneville, R. and McAllister, I. (2018). 'Gender, political knowledge, and descriptive representation: The impact of long-term socialization'. *American Journal of Political Science*, 62(2), 249–65.

Deschouwer, K. (2012). *The politics of Belgium: Governing a divided society.* Basingstoke: Palgrave Macmillan.

De Kamer (2021). 'Wetsvoorstel tot wijziging van de wet van 23 maart 1989 betreffende de verkiezing van het Europees parlement, teneinde de burgers vanaf de leeftijd van 16 jaar de mogelijkheid teg even om te gaan stemmen'. www.dekamer.be/FLWB/PDF/55/2373/55K2373001.pdf (last consulted on 27 December 2022).

De Standaard (2001). 'Niet gaan stemmen blijft strafbaar in Mechelen'. www .standaard.be/cnt/dst07022001_015.

De Vries, C. E., Hakhverdian, A., and Lancee, B. (2013). 'The dynamics of voters' left/right identification: The role of economic and cultural attitudes'. *Political Science Research and Methods*, 1(2), 223–38.

Delli Carpini, M. X. and Keeter, S. (1996). *What Americans know about politics and why it matters.* New Haven: Yale University Press.

DeNardo, J. (1980). 'Turnout and the vote: The joke's on the democrats'. *American Political Science Review*, 74(2), 406–20.

Eisinga, R., Te Grotenhuis, M., and Pelzer, B. (2012). 'Weather conditions and political party vote share in Dutch national parliament elections, 1971–2010'. *International Journal of Biometerology*, 56(6), 1161–5.

Engelen, B. (2005). 'Een dam tegen het leeglopen van de democratie: Pleidooi voor het behoud van de opkomstplicht'. *Ethiek en Maatschappij*, 8(2), 49–63.

Engelen, B. (2007). 'Why compulsory voting can enhance democracy'. *Acta Politica*, 42(1), 23–39.

Evans, T. (2006). *Compulsory voting in Australia.* Australian Electoral Commission Report. https://emailfooter.aec.gov.au/About_Aec/Publications/voting/files/compulsory-voting.pdf

Feitosa, F., Blais, A., and Dassonneville, R. (2020). 'Rules, politics, and policy'. *Election Law Journal*, 19, 19–44.

Ferwerda, J. (2014). 'Electoral consequences of declining participation: A natural experiment in Austria'. *Electoral Studies*, 35, 242–52.

Fornos, C. A., Power, T. J., and Garand, J. C. (2004). 'Explaining voter turnout in Latin America, 1980 to 2000'. *Comparative Political Studies*, 37(8), 909–40.

Fowler, A. (2013). 'Electoral and policy consequences of voter turnout: Evidence from compulsory voting in Australia'. *Quarterly Journal of Political Science*, 8(2), 159–82.

Franklin, M. (1999). 'Electoral engineering and cross-national turnout differences: What role for compulsory voting?' *British Journal of Political Science*, 29(1), 205–24.

Freire, A. and Turgeon, M. (2020). 'Random votes under compulsory voting: Evidence from Brazil'. *Electoral Studies*, 66, 102168.

Gallego, A. (2010). 'Understanding unequal turnout: Education and voting in comparative perspective'. *Electoral Studies*, 29(2), 239–48.

Gerlache, A. (2012). Tweet published on 11 October 2012. https://twitter.com/AlainGerlache/status/256324758625464320 (last accessed on 18 February 2022).

Geys, B. (2006). 'Explaining voter turnout: A review of aggregate-level research'. *Electoral Studies*, 25(4), 637–63.

Glasman, L. R. and Albarracín, D. (2006). 'Forming attitudes that predict future behavior: A meta-analysis of the attitude-behavior relation'. *Psychological Bulletin*, 132(5), 778–822.

Godbout, J.-F. and Turgeon, M. (2019). 'The preferences of voters and non-voters in Canada (1988–2008)'. In Loewen, P. J. and Rubenson, D. (eds.), *Duty and choice: The evolution of the study of voting and voters*. Toronto: University of Toronto Press, pp. 81–104.

Gomez, B. T., Hansford, T. G., and Krause, G. A. (2007). 'The Republicans should pray for rain: Weather, turnout and voting in US presidential elections'. *Journal of Politics*, 69(3), 649–63.

Gow, N. (1971). 'The introduction of compulsory voting in the Australian Commonwealth'. *Politics*, 6(2), 201–10.

Hill, L. (2006). 'Lower voter turnout in the United States: Is compulsory voting a viable solution?' *Journal of Theoretical Politics*, 18(2), 207–32.

Hirczy, W. (1994). 'The impact of mandatory voting laws on turnout: A quasi-experimental approach'. *Electoral Studies*, 13(1), 64–76.

Hirst, J. (2002). 'The distinctiveness of Australian democracy'. *Quadrant*, 46 (12), 19–27.

Hoffman, M., León, G., and Lombardi, M. (2017). 'Compulsory voting, turnout, and government spending: Evidence from Austria'. *Journal of Public Economics*, 145, 103–15.

Hooghe, L., and Marks, G. (2018). 'Cleavage theory meets Europe's crises: Lipset, Rokkan, and the transnational cleavage'. *Journal of European Public Policy*, 25(1), 109–35.

Hooghe, M. and Deschouwer, K. (2011). 'Veto players and electoral reform in Belgium'. *West European Politics*, 34(3), 626–43.

Hooghe, M. and Pelleriaux, K. (1998). 'Compulsory voting in Belgium: An application of the Lijphart thesis'. *Electoral Studies*, 17(4), 419–24.

IDEA (2021). 'Institute for democracy and electoral assistance voter turnout database'. www.idea.int/data-tools/data/voter-turnout (last accessed on 25 January 2021).

Irwin, G. (1974). 'Compulsory voting legislation, impact on voter turnout in the Netherlands'. *Comparative Political Studies*, 7(3), 292–315.

Jackman, S. (1999). 'Non-compulsory voting in Australia? What surveys can (and can't) tell us'. *Electoral Studies*, 18(1), 29–48.

Jackman, Simon (2001). Compulsory voting. In N. J. Smelser & B. Baltes (eds.), International Encyclopedia of the Social and Behavioral Sciences. pp. 16314–18.

Jaitman, L. (2013). 'The causal effect of compulsory voting laws on turnout: Does skill matter?' *Journal of Economic Behavior & Organization*, 92, 79–93.

Jensen, C. B. and Spoon, J.-J. (2011). 'Compelled without direction: Compulsory voting and party system spreading'. *Electoral Studies*, 30(4), 700–11.

Jerit, J. and Barabas, J. (2017). 'Revisiting the gender gap in political knowledge'. *Political Behavior*, 39(4), 817–38.

Kang, W. C. (2019). 'Liberals should pray for rain: Weather, opportunity costs of voting and electoral outcomes in South Korea'. *Political Science*, 71(1), 61–78.

Katz, G. and Levin, I. (2018). 'A general model of abstention under compulsory voting'. *Political Science Research and Methods*, 6(3), 489–508.

Kostelka, F., Shane, S., and Blais, A. (2021). 'Is compulsory voting a solution to low and declining turnout? Cross-national evidence since 1945'. forthcoming in Political Science Research and Methods DOI: https://doi.org/10.1017/psrm.2022.57.

Kouba, K. (2021). 'Where is the class bias attenuation? The consequences of adopting compulsory voting in Austria-Hungary in 1907'. *European Political Science Review*, 13(2), 151–167.

Kriesi, H., Grande, E., Lachat, R. et al. (2006). 'Globalization and the transformation of the national political space: Six European countries compared'. *European Journal of Political Research*, 45(6), 921–56.

Kropko, J. and Banda, K. K. (2018). 'Issue scales, information cues, and proximity and directional models of voter choice'. *Political Research Quarterly*, 71(4), 772–87.

Kuklinski, J. H., Quirk, P. J., Jerit, J., and Rich, R. F. (2001). 'The political environment and citizen competence'. *American Journal of Political Science*, 45(2), 410–24.

Kuzelewska, E. (2016). 'Compulsory voting in Belgium. A few remarks on mandatory voting'. *Bialstockie Studia Prawnicze*, 20, 37–51.

Lever, A. 2010. 'Compulsory voting: A critical perspective'. *British Journal of Political Science*, 40(4), 897–915.

Lijphart, A. (1997). 'Unequal participation: Democracy's unresolved dilemma'. *American Political Science Review*, 91(1), 1–14.

Lijphart, A. (2001). 'Compulsory voting is the best way to keep democracy strong'. In DiClerico, R. E. and Hammock, A. S. (eds.), *Points of view.* New York: McGraw Hill, pp. 74–7.

Love, J. L. (1970). 'Political participation in Brazil, 1881–1969'. *Luso-Brazilian Review*, 7(2), 3–24.

Lupu, N. and Warner, Z. (2021). 'Why are the affluent better represented around the world?' *European Journal of Political Research*, 61(1), 67–85.

Luskin, R. C. (1990). 'Explaining political sophistication'. *Political Behavior*, 12(4), 331–61.

Lutz, G. and Marsh, M. (2007). 'The consequences of low turnout'. *Electoral Studies*, 26(3), 539–47.

McAllister, I. (1986). 'Compulsory voting, turnout and party advantage in Australia'. *Politics*, 21(1), 89–93.

McAllister, I. and Snagovsky, F. (2018). 'Explaining voting in the 2017 Australian same sex marriage plebiscite'. *Australian Journal of Political Science*, 53(4), 409–27.

Mackerras, M. and McAllister, I. (1999). 'Compulsory voting, party stability and electoral advantage in Australia'. *Electoral Studies*, 18(2), 217–33.

Mainwaring, S. (1986). 'The transition to democracy in Brazil'. *Journal of Interamerican Studies and World Affairs*, 28(1), 141–79.

Malkopolou, A. (2014). *The history of compulsory voting in Europe: Democracy's duty?* London: Routledge.

Meier, P. (2012). 'Caught between strategic positions and principles of equality: Female suffrage in Belgium'. In Rodriguez Ruiz, B. and Rubio Marín, R. (eds.), *The struggle for female suffrage in Europe: Voting to become citizens.* Leiden: Brill, pp. 407–20.

Mellows, R. (2010). 'Compulsory voting just an illusion'. *Adelaide Advertiser*, 23 August, 18.

Miller, P. and Dassonneville, R. (2016). 'High turnout in the low countries: Partisan effects of the abolition of compulsory voting in the Netherlands'. *Electoral Studies*, 44, 132–43.

Nagel, J. and McNulty, J. (1996). 'Partisan effects of voter turnout in senatorial and gubernatorial elections'. *American Political Science Review*, 90(4), 780–93.

Oliveira, L. H. H. D. (1999). 'Voto obrigatório e eqüidade um estudo de caso'. *São Paulo em perspectiva*, 13, 144–52.

Oliveira, C. and Turgeon, M. (2015). 'Ideologia e comportamento politico no eleitorado brasileiro'. *Opinião Pública*, 21(3), 574–600.

Pacek, A. and Radcliff, B. (1995). 'Turnout and the vote for left-of-centre parties: A cross-national analysis'. *British Journal of Political Science*, 25 (1), 137–43.

Panagopoulos, C. (2008). 'The calculus of voting in compulsory voting systems'. *Political Behavior*, 30(4), 455–67.

Pattie, C. and Johnston, R. (1998). 'Voter turnout at the British general election of 1992: Rational choice, social standing or political efficacy?' *European Journal of Political Research*, 33(2), 263–83.

Pilet, J. B. (2007). 'Choosing compulsory voting in Belgium: Strategy and ideas combined'. In *ECPR Joint Sessions of Workshops*, Helsinki.

Power, T. J. (2000). 'Democratic Brazil. Politics as permanent constitutional convention'. In Kingstone P. R. and Power T. J. (eds.), *Democratic Brazil: Actors, institutions, and processes*. Pittsburgh: University of Pittsburgh Press, pp. 17–35.

Power, T. J. and Roberts, J. T. (1995). 'Compulsory voting, invalid ballots, and abstention in Brazil'. *Political Research Quarterly*, 48(3), 795–826.

Pringle, H. (2012). 'Compulsory voting in Australia: What is compulsory?' *Australian Journal of Political Science*, 47(3), 427–40.

Remer-Bollow, U., Bernhagen, P., and Rose, R. (2019). 'Partisan consequences of low turnout at elections to the European Parliament'. *Electoral Studies*, 59, 87–98.

Reuchamps, M., Devillers, S., Caluwaerts, D., and Bouhon, F. (2018). 'Le vote obligatoire'. In Bouhon, F. and Reuchamps, M. (eds.), *Les systèmes électoraux de la Belgique*. Brussels: Bruylant, pp. 403–22.

Ricci, P. and Zulini, J. P. (2017). 'The politics of electoral reforms: The origins of proportional representation in Brazil and the electoral code of 1932'. In J. George and L. Rennó (eds.), *Institutional innovation and the steering of conflicts in Latin America*. Colchester: ECPR Press, pp. 57–84.

Rios, F. (2020). 'Cycles of democracy and the racial issue in Brazil (1978–2019)'. In Bianchi, B., Chaloub, J., Rangel, P., and Wolf, F. O. (eds.), *Democracy and Brazil: Collapse and regression*. New York: Routledge, pp. 26–40.

Rubenson, D., Blais, A., Fournier, P., Gidengil, E., and Nevitte, N. (2007). 'Does low turnout matter? Evidence from the 2000 Canadian federal election'. *Electoral Studies*, 26(3), 589–97.

Rudolph, L. (2020). 'Turning out to turn down the EU: The mobilisation of occasional voters and Brexit'. *Journal of European Public Policy*, 27(12), 1858–78.

Rychter, T. (2018). 'How compulsory voting works: Australians explain'. Published in the *New York Times* on 22 October 2018. www.nytimes.com/

2018/10/22/world/australia/compulsory-voting.html (last accessed on 18 February 2022).

Selb, P. and Lachat, R. (2009). 'The more, the better? Counterfactual evidence on the effect of compulsory voting on the consistency of party choice'. *European Journal of Political Research*, 48(5), 573–97.

Selb, P. and Munzert, S. (2013). 'Voter overrepresentation, vote misreporting, and turnout bias in postelection surveys'. *Electoral Studies*, 32(1), 186–96.

Senate (2012). 'Commissie voor de justie: Handelingen'. Commissihandelingen nr. 5–178. www.senate.be/www/?MIval=/consulteren/publicatie2& BLOKNR=9&COLL=C&LEG=5&NR=178&SUF=&VOLGNR=&LANG=nl (last consulted on 25 January 2022).

Sheppard, J. (2015). 'Compulsory voting and political knowledge: Testing a "compelled engagement" hypothesis'. *Electoral Studies*, 40, 300–7.

Shineman, V. (2021). 'Isolating the effect of compulsory voting laws on political sophistication: Leveraging intra-national variation in mandatory voting laws between the Austrian Provinces'. *Electoral Studies*, 71, 102265.

Singh, S. (2010). 'Contextual influences on the decision calculus: A cross-national examination of proximity voting'. *Electoral Studies*, 29(3), 425–34.

Singh, S. (2011). 'How compelling is compulsory voting? A multilevel analysis of turnout'. *Political Behavior*, 33(1), 95–111.

Singh, S. (2015). 'Compulsory voting and the turnout decision calculus'. *Political Studies*, 63(3), 548–68.

Singh, S. (2018). 'Compulsory voting and dissatisfaction with democracy'. *British Journal of Political Science*, 48(3), 843–54.

Singh, S. (2019). Compulsory voting and parties' vote-seeking strategies. *American Journal of Political Science*, 63(1), 37–52.

Singh, S. (2021). *Beyond turnout: How compulsory voting shapes citizens and political parties*. Oxford: Oxford University Press.

Slovak, M. and Vassil, K. (2015). 'Indifference or Indignation? Explaining purposive vote spoiling in elections'. *Journal of Elections, Public Opinion and Parties*, 25(4), 463–81.

Smets, K. and Van Ham, C. (2013). 'The embarrassment of riches? A meta-analysis of individual-level research on voter turnout'. *Electoral Studies*, 32(2), 344–59.

Söderlund, P., Wass, H., and Blais, A. (2011). 'The impact of motivational and contextual factors on turnout in first- and second-order elections'. *Electoral Studies*, 30(4), 689–99.

Stengers, J. (1990). 'Histoire de la législation électorale en Belgique'. In Noiret, S. (ed.), *Stratégies politiques et réformes électorales aux origines des modes de scrutin en Europe aux XIXe et XXe sièglés*. Baden Baden: Nomos Verlagsgesellschaft, pp. 76–107.

Stockemer, D. (2017). 'What affects voter turnout? A review article/meta-analysis of aggregate research'. *Government and Opposition*, 52(4), 698–722.

Strangio, P. (2021). '"A lonely and quixotic battle": A short history of agitation against compulsory voting in Australia'. In Bonotti, M. and Strangio, P. (eds.), *A century of compulsory voting in Australia: Genesis, impact and future*. Basingstoke: Palgrave Macmillan, pp. 33–57.

Sudinfo (2014). 'Vous n'allez pas voter? La justice belge n'applique pas de loi sur l'obligation de vote'. www.sudinfo.be/art/1006451/article/2014-05-14/vous-n-allez-pas-voter-la-justice-belge-n-applique-pas-la-loi-sur-l-obligation-d (last consulted on 25 January 2022).

Superior Electoral Court (2023). 'Election statistics'. https://sig.tse.jus.br/ords/dwapr/seai/r/sig-eleicao-comp-abst/faixa-et%C3%A1ria?session=2127038 02525676 (last consulted on 12 January 2023).

Turgeon, M. and Blais, A. (2021). 'Am I obliged to vote? A regression discontinuity analysis of compulsory voting with ill-Informed voters'. *Political Science Research and Methods*, 11.1 (2023), 207–13.

van der Brug, W. and Rekker, R. (2021). 'Dealignment, realignment and generational differences in the Netherlands'. *West European Politics*, 44(4), 776–80.

Victorian Electoral Commission (2015). 'Report to the Parliament on the 2014 State election'. https://parliament.vic.gov.au/file_uploads/Report_to_Parliament_on_2014_Vic_election-CD_xT1f9RWG.pdf (last consulted on 25 January 2022).

Vlaamse Overheid (2021). 'Voorontwerp van decreet tot wijziging van diverse decreten wat betreft versterking van de locale democratie'. VR 2021 3004 DOC.0468/3. https://beslissingenvlaamseregering.vlaanderen.be/document-view/6087B9E6364ED90008000954 (last consulted on 25 January 2022).

Volacu, A. (2020). 'Democracy and compulsory voting'. *Political Research Quarterly*, 73(2), 454–63.

VRT Nieuws (2018). 'Hoe moet u stemmen? Wat moet, wat mag, wat mag niet?' www.vrt.be/vrtnws/nl/drafts/Politiek/hoe-moet-u-stemmen-wat-moet-wat-mag-wat-mag-niet/.

Zulini, J. P. and Ricci, P. (2020). 'O Código Eleitoral de 1932 e as eleições da Era Vargas: um passo na direção da democracia?'. *Estudos Históricos (Rio de Janeiro)*, 33, 600–23.

Cambridge Elements ≡

Campaigns and Elections

R. Michael Alvarez

California Institute of Technology

R. Michael Alvarez is Professor of Political and Computational Social Science at Caltech. His current research focuses on election administration and technology, campaigns and elections, and computational modeling.

Emily Beaulieu Bacchus

University of Kentucky

Emily Beaulieu Bacchus is Associate Professor of Political Science and Director of International Studies at the University of Kentucky. She is an expert in political institutions and contentious politics – focusing much of her work on perceptions of election fraud and electoral protests. Electoral Protest and Democracy in the Developing World was published with Cambridge University Press in 2014.

Charles Stewart III

Massachusetts Institute of Technology

Charles Stewart III is the Kenan Sahin Distinguished Professor of Political Science at MIT. His research and teaching focus on American politics, election administration, and legislative politics.

About the Series

Broadly focused, covering electoral campaigns & strategies, voting behavior, and electoral institutions, this Elements series offers the opportunity to publish work from new and emerging fields, especially those at the interface of technology, elections, and global electoral trends.

Cambridge Elements ☰

Campaigns and Elections

Elements in the Series

Printed in the United States
by Baker & Taylor Publisher Services